PROFESSIONAL FOUNDATIONS

Learning Strategies

PF 321

contains selected material from

Interpersonal Skills in Organizations

Suzanne C. De Janasz, Ph.D.
University of Mary Washington

Karen O. Dowd, Ph.D.
James Madison University

Beth Z. Schneider, MBA
George Mason University

College Writing Skills with Readings, Sixth Edition

John Langan
Atlantic Cape Community College

A Writer's Resource: A Handbook for Writing and Research

Elaine P. Maimon
Arizona State University West

Janice H. Peritz
*Queens College,
City University of New York*

D1417952

McGraw Hill Custom Publishing

Boston   Burr Ridge, IL   Dubuque, IA   Madison, WI   New York
San Francisco   St. Louis   Bangkok   Bogotá   Caracas   Kuala Lumpur
Lisbon   London   Madrid   Mexico City   Milan   Montreal   New Delhi
Santiago   Seoul   Singapore   Sydney   Taipei   Toronto

PROFESSIONAL FOUNDATIONS
Learning Strategies
PF 321

This book is a McGraw-Hill Custom Publishing textbook and contains select material from
Interpersonal Skills in Organizations by Suzanne C. De Janasz, Karen O. Dowd, and Beth Z. Schneider. Copyright ©2006, 2002 by The McGraw-Hill Companies, Inc.
College Writing Skills with Readings, Sixth Edition by John Langan. Copyright © 2005, 2001, 1997, 1993, 1989, 1985 by The McGraw-Hill Companies, Inc.
A Writer's Resource: A Handbook for Writing and Research by Elaine P. Maimon and Janice H. Peritz. Copyright © 2003 by The McGraw-Hill Companies, Inc.
Reprinted with permission of the publisher. Many custom published texts are modified versions or adaptations of our best-selling textbooks. Some adaptations are printed in black and white to keep prices at a minimum, while others are in color.

4 5 6 7 8 9 0 MER   MER   0 9 8 7 6

ISBN 0–256-29718-5

Editor: Tamara Immell
Production Editor: Carrie Braun
Cover Design: Maggie Lytle
Cover Photographer: Computer–Ryan McVay/Getty Images
Printer/Binder: Mercury Print Productions

Contents

Bad Writing Always
Leaves Negative Impressions

Mar. 14--Rather than serving as a calling card that helps get your foot in the door, a poorly written resume may ensure that the door stays slammed shut.

Yet, Frank Nero, president and chief executive of the Beacon Council -- Miami-Dade's economic development agency, says he has seen far too many resumes that are poorly written.

"I come across many resumes and applications that are rather shocking," Nero said. "They don't follow the proper format and have misspellings and grammar errors. [Applicants] can't even write a cover letter."

Writing matters and many business leaders in South Florida say sending clear and concise written messages to customers and global clients is a top priority. But they also say it's not easy to find employees with good written communications skills.

"Here we have a worldwide audience, and sadly these are dying skills," said Nero.

A report published last year by the National Commission on Writing for America's Families, Schools and Colleges concluded that the ability to communicate and write well opens doors to professional employment and promotions in all business sectors.

The study, Writing: A Ticket to Work. . .Or a Ticket Out, A Survey of Business Leaders, surveyed 120 human resource directors in companies affiliated with Business Roundtable, an association of chief executives officers from U.S. corporations with a combined workforce of more than 10 million employees.

With e-mail replacing the phone for much workplace communication, being concise, clear and having good grammar are among the top requisites that employers seek in applicants.

But Marcus Elosegui, a branch manager at Personally Yours Staffing, a personnel service firm with offices in Miami-Dade, Broward and Palm Beach counties, sees a number of writing deficiencies among local job applicants. They include grammar problems, the use of slang in written proposals and a lack of familiarity with the terms specific to various industries.

"We screen applicants that have been working in the legal, real estate and medical sectors for years," said Elosegui. "We administer tests to check their spelling and grammar. A lot of people who apply for top-level positions can't even spell terms they use every day."

Elosegui also observed that there are a great number of executives in South Florida who claim to be bilingual but are not as fluent and proficient in their second language as they say.

"Here we have people from other countries that are really qualified to take a position but are lacking grammar and speech skills," said Elosegui in a phone interview. "We recently had two excellent candidates for a position of executive assistant at a financial firm, but their writing and speaking deficiencies -- because of the language barrier -- kept them from getting the job."

The firm's clients, who include Tropicana and Goya Food Products, are "very demanding when it comes to language and grammar," Elosegui said.

The problem of poor writing skills also extends to the college campus.

Kevin Hall, an editor-in-residence and associate professor of the School of Mass Communications at Florida International University, said language skills suffered after a massive influx of Hispanic immigrants in the 1980s overwhelmed the school system.

Like many professionals, Hall complains the region is becoming bi-illiterate.

Schools and universities "do not teach the fundamentals of the English language properly, and people are not studying Spanish. So individuals do not have a conscious relationship with either language," he said.

"The ability to communicate ideas clearly is crucial to succeed," said Hall, a former journalist and writing consultant.

The report by the National Commission on Writing for America's Families, Schools and Colleges said that businesses across the United States are spending as much as $3.1 billion annually in remedial training to improve the language and writing of employees.

But even more of an effort is needed, said Hall.

"Corporations try, but a two-day seminar is not going to accomplish anything. It is money being wasted. Improvement can only be achieved over long periods of time. The business community needs to demand more from schools to prepare kids."

At FIU, all undergraduate students at the College of Business are required to take a three-credit course called "Business and Professional Communication," said Brian Schriner, a communications professor at the business school.

"We teach the proper formats and style," said Schriner. "Students usually write in academic style, taught to them in history and philosophy classes. But business writing is extremely practical," he said.

In the course, students learn business-writing techniques, how to prepare oral presentations, critical thinking and team thinking.

"The problem with professionals and writing is that sometimes they don't know how to get to the point . . . letters and e-mails are sometimes too wordy," Schriner said. "E-mails are normally used for personal purposes, so they tend to be informal. [But in a professional context,] managers have higher expectations and they expect e-mails and reports to be complete, clear and courteous."

Schriner said that in his course he is "reinforcing the fundamentals" students already have.

Some said, however, that they hadn't had any formal grammar education since they were in elementary school. They found the course helpful.

"In my job, I'm able to see results," said Mike Pintado, 22, who works at Tropex Construction Services. "When I write a fax letter that is only three lines long, I realize that it's very short but all the information is there. That's because we're used to writing essays and long papers."

Schriner's Tuesday session includes four international students from Taiwan, Israel, Mexico and Nicaragua who don't count English as their first language.

For Jorge Santos Coy, a student from Mexico, the course is especially helpful. "This course is the key that opens the door to professional writing," he said.

To see more of The Miami Herald -- including its homes, jobs, cars and other classified listings -- or to subscribe to the newspaper, go to http://www.herald.com.

Source: Miami Herald, The (FL), Mar 14, 2005
Item: 2W63426725408

Job Offers Go to Those with Classic Skills

Job seekers have found a significant upswing in the employment market over the past 12 months. Recruiting traffic at university career centers and postings on Internet job boards have increased markedly. Through this growth, it's been interesting to speak to hiring managers and corporate recruiters who visit the Iowa State University College of Business about what traits define the "best" candidate.

Over the past decade – while technology and business practices have changed dramatically – the critical candidate traits identified by hiring managers as being most important have not changed much at all.

So what basic traits define the best candidate in a search? Are the skills you seek from job candidates in sync with the skills demanded by other employers: Hiring managers consistently identify a general set of desired characteristics that are fairly universal across industries, organizations and position levels. They are:

Common skills – Nearly every listing of desired traits published in surveys, as well as virtually every conversation with hiring managers, places communication skills as the first criterion for candidate evaluation. Solid communication skills are fundamentally critical for every aspect of business, and employers note the strong direct connection between excellent communication and performance in the workplace. Job candidates must demonstrate their written and verbal communication at several points in the job-search process, from offering up an error-free and effectively written resume and cover letter, to handling the interview process with sophistication.

Leadership – The ability to lead People and teams is important even in entry-level jobs, and becomes increasingly critical as one's career advances. In the interview process, recruiters and hiring managers seek specific examples that demonstrate candidates' leadership experience and capabilities. They usually do this by asking "behavioral interview" questions designed to explore specific situations in which a candidate has interacted with people and groups, in order to identify the candidate's leadership experience and potential.

Teamwork – Again using behavioral interview techniques, hiring managers seek candidates who can demonstrate that they have experience collaborating in organizations to achieve successful results.

Computer literacy – This one is pretty straightforward. What do we do in the business world today without a computer? Not much. Knowledge of the Microsoft Office suite is the bare minimum expectation today. Of course, many positions require some sort of additional specific computer knowledge and experience.

Analytical skills – Nearly all hiring managers want candidates who can demonstrate the ability to analyze and solve problems. Again, the emphasis is on demonstrate. It's not enough for candidates to state that they have analytical ability; they must be prepared to offer specific results-driven examples to illustrate.

Of course, all jobs have additional specific skill or knowledge requirements. These may include technical expertise, quantitative knowledge or particular experience. Hiring managers will also closely evaluate a candidate's perceived fit with the organization's culture, evidence of adaptability and whether the candidate has proven ability to perform.

An M.B.A. degree can boost a candidate's abilities in these latter areas. But hiring managers also make clear that among the key reasons they seek M.B.A. graduates for many positions is that they demonstrate superior abilities in effective communication, leadership, team skills and analytical prowess, in addition to specific function content.

6

Grammar

23 Subjects and Verbs

The basic building blocks of English sentences are subjects and verbs. Understanding them is an important first step toward mastering a number of sentence skills.

Every sentence has a subject and a verb. Who or what the sentence speaks about is called the *subject;* what the sentence says about the subject is called the *verb.* In the following sentences, the subject is underlined once and the verb twice.

The boy cried.

That fish smells.

Many people applied for the job.

The show is a documentary.

A Simple Way to Find a Subject

To find a subject, ask *who* or *what* the sentence is about. As shown below, your answer is the subject.

Who is the first sentence about? The boy

What is the second sentence about? That fish

Who is the third sentence about? Many people

What is the fourth sentence about? The show

A Simple Way to Find a Verb

14.1c

To find a verb, ask what the sentence *says about* the subject. As shown below, your answer is the verb.

What does the first sentence *say about* the boy? He cried.

What does the second sentence *say about* the fish? It smells.

Handbook of Sentence Skills

What does the third sentence *say about* the people? They applied.

What does the fourth sentence *say about* the show? It is a documentary.

A second way to find the verb is to put *I, you, he, she, it,* or *they* in front of the word you think is a verb. If the result makes sense, you have a verb. For example, you could put *he* in front of *cried* in the first sentence above, with the result, *he cried,* making sense. Therefore, you know that *cried* is a verb. You could use the same test with the other three verbs as well.

Finally, it helps to remember that most verbs show action. In the sentences already considered, the three action verbs are *cried, smells,* and *applied.* Certain other verbs, known as *linking verbs,* do not show action. They do, however, give information about the subject. In The show is a doc umentary," the linking verb *is* joins the subject (*show*) with a word that identifies or describes it (*documentary*). Other common linking verbs include *am, are, was, were, feel, appear, look, become,* and *seem.*

ACTIVITY

In each of the following sentences, draw one line under the subject and two lines under the verb.

1. The ripening tomatoes glistened on the sunny windowsill.
2. Acupuncture reduces the pain of my headaches.
3. Elena twisted a strand of hair around her fingers.
4. My brother built his bookshelves from cinder blocks and wood planks.
5. A jackrabbit bounds up to fifteen feet in one leap.
6. The singer's diamond earrings sparkled in the spotlight.
7. My roommate crashed his car on the icy highway.
8. On St. Patrick's Day, our neighborhood tavern serves green beer.
9. My six-year-old brother survives on a diet of peanut butter and jelly.
10. During my parents' divorce, I felt like a rag doll being torn between two people.

More about Subjects and Verbs

18.1

1 A sentence may have more than one verb, more than one subject, or several subjects and verbs.

The engine coughed and sputtered.

Subjects and Verbs

Broken <u>glass</u> and empty <u>cans</u> <u>littered</u> the parking lot.

<u>Marta</u>, <u>Nilsa</u>, and <u>Robert</u> <u>met</u> after class and <u>headed</u> downtown.

2   The subject of the sentence never appears within a prepositional phrase. A *prepositional phrase* is simply a group of words that begins with a preposition. Following is a list of common prepositions.

Prepositions				
about	before	by	inside	over
above	behind	during	into	through
across	below	except	like	to
among	beneath	for	of	toward
around	beside	from	off	under
at	between	in	on, onto	with

Crossing out prepositional phrases will help you find the subject or subjects of a sentence.

A <u>stream</u> of cold air <u>seeps</u> in through the space below the door.

<u>Specks</u> of dust <u>dance</u> gently in a ray of sunlight.

The <u>people</u> in the apartment above ours <u>fight</u> loudly.

The murky <u>waters</u> of the polluted lake <u>spilled</u> over the dam.

The amber <u>lights</u> on its sides <u>outlined</u> the tractor-trailer in the hazy dusk.

3   Many verbs consist of more than one word. (The extra verbs are called *auxiliary,* or *helping,* verbs.) Here, for example, are some of the many forms of the verb *work.*

Forms of work		
work	worked	should work
works	were working	will be working
does work	have worked	can work
is working	had worked	could be working
are working	had been working	must have worked

Handbook of Sentence Skills

4   Words like *not, just, never, only,* and *always* are not part of the verb, although they may appear within the verb.

Ruby has never liked cold weather.
Our boss will not be singing with the choir this year.
The intersection has not always been this dangerous.

5   A verb preceded by *to* is never the verb of a sentence.

At night, my son likes to read under the covers.
Evelyn decided to separate from her husband.

6   An *-ing* word by itself is never the verb of a sentence. (It may be part of the verb, but it must have a helping verb in front of it.)

They going on a trip this weekend.
(not a sentence, because the verb is not complete)

They are going on a trip this weekend. (a sentence)

ACTIVITY

Draw a single line under subjects and a double line under verbs. Cross out prepositional phrases as necessary to find the subjects.

1. A thick layer of dust covers the top of our refrigerator.
2. In June, sagging Christmas decorations were still hanging in the windows of the abandoned house.
3. The people in the all-night coffee shop seemed weary and lost.
4. Every plant in the dim room bent toward the small window.
5. A glaring headline about the conviction of a local congressman attracted my attention.
6. Two of the biggest stores in the mall are going out of business.
7. The battery tester's tiny red lights suddenly started to flicker.
8. A neighbor of mine does all her work at home and e-mails it to her office.
9. The jar of peppercorns tumbled from the spice shelf and shattered on the floor.
10. The scar in the hollow of Brian's throat is the result of an emergency operation to clear his windpipe.

■ Review Test

Draw a single line under subjects and a double line under verbs. Cross out prepositional phrases as necessary to find the subjects.

1. With one graceful motion, the shortstop fielded the grounder and threw to first base.

2. Like human mothers, sheep and goat mothers develop close bonds with their babies.

3. Before class, Antonietta and Jorge rushed to the coffee machine in the hall.

4. I shifted uncomfortably on the lumpy mattress before falling into a restless sleep.

5. Waiting in the long ticket line, Matt shifted his weight from one foot to the other.

6. Ancient Egyptians were branding cattle more than four thousand years ago.

7. Dogs and cats crowded the veterinarian's office on Monday morning.

8. The driver abruptly halted her Jeep and backed up toward a narrow parking place.

9. During the American Revolution, some brides rejected white wedding gowns and wore red as a symbol of rebellion.

10. The little girl's frantic family called a psychic to locate the child.

24 Fragments

Every sentence must have a subject and a verb and must express a complete thought. A word group that lacks a subject or a verb and does not express a complete thought is a *fragment*. Following are the most common types of fragments that people write:

1   Dependent-word fragments
2   *-ing* and *to* fragments
3   Added-detail fragments
4   Missing-subject fragments

Once you understand what specific kinds of fragments you might write, you should be able to eliminate them from your writing. The following pages explain all four types.

Dependent-Word Fragments

Some word groups that begin with a dependent word are fragments. Following is a list of common dependent words. Whenever you start a sentence with one of these words, you must be careful that a fragment does not result.

Dependent Words

after	if, even if	when, whenever
although, though	in order that	where, wherever
as	since	whether
because	that, so that	which, whichever
before	unless	while
even though	until	who
how	what, whatever	whose

In the example below, the word group beginning with the dependent word *after* is a fragment:

After I cashed my paycheck. I treated myself to dinner.

A *dependent statement*—one starting with a dependent word like *after*—cannot stand alone. It depends on another statement to complete the thought. *After I cashed my paycheck* is a dependent statement. It leaves us hanging. We expect to find out, in the same sentence, *what happened after* the writer cashed the check. When a writer does not follow through and complete a thought, a fragment results.

To correct the fragment, simply follow through and complete the thought:

After I cashed my paycheck, I treated myself to dinner.

Remember, then, that *dependent statements by themselves are fragments.* They must be attached to a statement that makes sense standing alone.

Here are two other examples of dependent-word fragments.

I won't leave the house. Until I hear from you.

Rick finally picked up the socks. That he had thrown on the floor days ago.

Until I hear from you is a fragment; it does not make sense standing by itself. We want to know in the same statement *what cannot happen* until I hear from you. The writer must complete the thought. Likewise, *That he had thrown on the floor days ago* is not in itself a complete thought. We want to know in the same statement what *that* refers to.

How to Correct a Dependent-Word Fragment

In most cases you can correct a dependent-word fragment by attaching it to the sentence that comes after it or the sentence that comes before it:

After I cashed my paycheck, I treated myself to dinner.
(The fragment has been attached to the sentence that comes after it.)

I won't leave the house until I hear from you.
(The fragment has been attached to the sentence that comes before it.)

Rick finally picked up the socks that he had thrown on the floor days ago.
(The fragment has been attached to the sentence that comes before it.)

Handbook of Sentence Skills

Another way of correcting a dependent-word fragment is simply to eliminate the dependent word by rewriting the sentence.

I cashed my paycheck and then treated myself to dinner.
I will wait to hear from you.
He had thrown them on the floor days ago.

Notes

a Use a comma if a dependent word group comes at the *beginning* of a sentence (see also page 516):

After I cashed my paycheck, I treated myself to dinner.

However, do not generally use a comma if the dependent word group comes at the *end* of a sentence.

I won't leave the house until I hear from you.
Rick finally picked up the socks that he had thrown on the floor days ago.

b Sometimes the dependent words *who, that, which,* or *where* appear not at the very start but *near* the start of a word group. A fragment often results:

I drove slowly past the old brick house. The place where I grew up.

The place where I grew up is not in itself a complete thought. We want to know in the same statement *where was the place* the writer grew up. The fragment can be corrected by attaching it to the sentence that comes before it:

I drove slowly past the old brick house, the place where I grew up.

ACTIVITY 1

Turn each of the following dependent word groups into a sentence by adding a complete thought. Use a comma after the dependent word group if a dependent word starts the sentence. Note the examples.

EXAMPLES   Although I felt miserable

Although I felt miserable, I tried to smile for the photographer.

The man who found my wallet

The man who found my wallet returned it the next day.

Fragments

1. If I don't get a raise soon

   _____

   _____

2. Because it was raining

   _____

   _____

3. When I heard the news

   _____

   _____

4. Because I couldn't find the car keys

   _____

   _____

5. The restaurant that we tried

   _____

   _____

ACTIVITY 2

Underline the dependent-word fragment in each item. Then rewrite the items, correcting each fragment by attaching it to the sentence that comes before or the sentence that comes after it—whichever sounds more natural. Use a comma after the dependent word group if it starts the sentence.

1. Whenever I spray deodorant. My cat arches her back. She thinks she is hearing a hissing enemy.

   _____

   _____

2. My father, a salesman, was on the road all week. We had a great time playing football in the house. Until he came home for the weekend.

   _____

   _____

3. If Kim takes too long saying good-bye to her boyfriend. Her father will start flicking the porch light. Then he will come out with a flashlight.

   _____

   _____

4. Scientists are studying mummified remains. That are thousands of years old. Most of the people were killed by parasites.

_____

_____

5. After I got to class. I realized my report was still on the kitchen table. I had been working there the night before.

_____

_____

-*ing* and *to* Fragments

When an -*ing* word appears at or near the start of a word group, a fragment may result. Such fragments often lack a subject and part of the verb. In the items below, underline the word groups that contain -*ing* words. Each is a fragment.

1. Ellen walked all over the neighborhood yesterday. Trying to find her dog Bo. Several people claimed they had seen him only hours before.
2. We sat back to watch the movie. Not expecting anything special. To our surprise, we clapped, cheered, and cried for the next two hours.
3. I telephoned the balloon store. It being the day before our wedding anniversary. I knew my wife would be surprised to receive a dozen heart-shaped balloons.

People sometimes write -*ing* fragments because they think that the subject of one sentence will work for the next word group as well. Thus, in item 1 the writer thinks that the subject *Ellen* in the opening sentence will also serve as the subject for *Trying to find her dog Bo.* But the subject must actually be in the same sentence.

How to Correct -*ing* Fragments

1 Attach the fragment to the sentence that comes before it or the sentence that comes after it, whichever makes sense. Item 1 could read: "Ellen walked all over the neighborhood yesterday trying to find her dog Bo."

2 Add a subject and change the -*ing* verb part to the correct form of the verb. Item 2 could read: "We didn't expect anything special."

3 Change *being* to the correct form of the verb *be (am, are, is, was, were)*. Item 3 could read: "It was the day before our wedding anniversary."

How to Correct *to* Fragments

When *to* appears at or near the start of a word group, a fragment sometimes results:

> At the Chinese restaurant, Tim used chopsticks. To impress his date. He spent one hour eating a small bowl of rice.

The second word group is a fragment and can be corrected by adding it to the preceding sentence:

> At the Chinese restaurant, Tim used chopsticks to impress his date.

ACTIVITY 1

Underline the *-ing* fragment in each of the following items. Then correct the item by using the method described in parentheses.

EXAMPLE Stepping hard on the accelerator. Armon tried to beat the truck to the intersection. He lost by a hood.
(Add the fragment to the sentence that comes after it.)

Stepping hard on the accelerator, Armon tried to beat the truck to

the intersection.

1. Marble-sized hailstones fell from the sky. Flattening the young plants in the cornfield. A year's work was lost in an hour.
(Add the fragment to the preceding sentence.)

_____

_____

2. A noisy fire truck suddenly raced down the street. Coming to a stop at my house. My home security system had sent a false alarm.
(Correct the fragment by adding the subject *it* and changing *coming* to the proper form of the verb, *came.*)

_____

_____

3. My phone doesn't ring. Instead, a light on it blinks. The reason for this being that I am partially deaf.
(Correct the fragment by changing *being* to the proper form of the verb, *is.*)

_____

_____

Handbook of Sentence Skills

ACTIVITY 2

Underline the *-ing* or *to* fragment in each item. Then rewrite each item, correcting the fragment by using one of the three methods described above.

1. Looking at the worm on the table. Shelby groaned. She knew she wouldn't like what the biology teacher said next.

   _____

   _____

2. I put a box of baking soda in the freezer. To get rid of the musty smell. However, my ice cubes still taste like old socks.

   _____

   _____

3. Staring at the clock on the far wall. I nervously began my speech. I was afraid to look at any of the people in the room.

   _____

   _____

4. Jerome sat quietly at his desk. Fantasizing about the upcoming weekend. He might meet the girl of his dreams at Saturday night's party.

   _____

   _____

5. To get to the bus station from here. You have to walk two blocks out of your way. The sidewalk is torn up because of construction work.

   _____

   _____

Added-Detail Fragments

Added-detail fragments lack a subject and a verb. They often begin with one of the following words:

also	especially	except	for example	like	including	such as

Fragments

Underline the one added-detail fragment in each of the following items:

1. Before a race, I eat starchy foods. Such as bread and spaghetti. The carbohydrates provide quick energy.
2. Bob is taking a night course in auto mechanics. Also, one in plumbing. He wants to save money on household repairs.
3. My son keeps several pets in his room. Including hamsters and mice.

People often write added-detail fragments for much the same reason they write *-ing* fragments. They think the subject and verb in one sentence will serve for the next word group. But the subject and verb must be in *each* word group.

How to Correct Added-Detail Fragments

1 Attach the fragment to the complete thought that precedes it. Item 1 could read: "Before a race, I eat starchy foods such as bread and spaghetti."

2 Add a subject and a verb to the fragment to make it a complete sentence. Item 2 could read: "Bob is taking a night course in auto mechanics. Also, he is taking one in plumbing."

3 Insert the fragment within the preceding sentence. Item 3 could read: "My son keeps several pets, including hamsters and mice, in his room."

ACTIVITY 1

Underline the fragment in each of the following items. Then make it a sentence by rewriting it, using the method described in parentheses.

EXAMPLE My mother likes watching daytime television shows. Especially old movies and soap operas. She says that daytime television is less violent. (Add the fragment to the preceding sentence.)

My mother likes watching daytime television shows, especially old movies and soap operas.

1. Luis works evenings in a video store. He enjoys the fringe benefits. For example, seeing the new movies first.
(Correct the fragment by adding the subject and verb *he sees*.)

_____

_____

2. Bob's fingernails are ragged from years of working as a mechanic. And his fingertips are always black. Like ink pads.
(Attach the fragment to the preceding sentence.)

_____

_____

3. Electronic devices keep getting smaller. Such as video cameras and cell phones. Some are so tiny they look like toys.
(Correct the fragment by inserting it in the preceding sentence.)

_____

_____

ACTIVITY 2

Underline the added-detail fragment in each item. Then rewrite to correct the fragment. Use one of the three methods described above.

1. Left-handed students face problems. For example, right-handed desks. Spiral notebooks can also be uncomfortable to use.

_____

_____

2. Mrs. Fields always wears her lucky clothes to bingo. Such as a sweater printed with four-leaf clovers. She also carries a rhinestone horseshoe.

_____

_____

3. Hundreds of moths were swarming around the stadium lights. Like large flecks of snow. However, I knew they couldn't be snow—it was eighty degrees outside.

_____

_____

4. Trevor buys and sells paper collectors' items. For instance, comic books and movie posters. He sets up a display at local flea markets and carnivals.

_____

_____

5. I wonder now why I had to learn certain subjects. Such as geometry. No one has ever asked me about the hypotenuse of a triangle.

_____

_____

Missing-Subject Fragments

In each item below, underline the word group in which the subject is missing:

1. Alicia loved getting wedding presents. But hated writing thank-you notes.
2. Mickey has orange soda and potato chips for breakfast. Then eats more junk food, like root beer and cookies, for lunch.

How to Correct Missing-Subject Fragments

1 Attach the fragment to the preceding sentence. Item 1 could read: "Alicia loved getting wedding presents but hated writing thank-you notes."

2 Add a subject (which can often be a pronoun standing for the subject in the preceding sentence). Item 2 could read: "Then he eats more junk food, like root beer and cookies, for lunch."

ACTIVITY

Underline the missing-subject fragment in each item. Then rewrite that part of the item needed to correct the fragment. Use one of the two methods of correction described above.

1. Every other day, Kara runs two miles. Then does fifty sit-ups. She hasn't lost weight, but she looks trimmer and more muscular.

   _____

   _____

2. I like all kinds of fresh pizza. But refuse to eat frozen pizza. The sauce is always dried out, and the crust tastes like leather.

   _____

   _____

3. Many people are allergic to seafood. They break out in hives when they eat it. And can even have trouble breathing.

   _____

   _____

4. To distract me, the dentist tugged at a corner of my mouth. Then jabbed a needle into my gums and injected a painkiller. I hardly felt it.

   _____

   _____

5. Last semester, I took six courses. And worked part-time in a discount drugstore. Now that the term is all over, I don't know how I did it.

_____

_____

A Review: How to Check for Sentence Fragments

1   Read your paper aloud from the *last* sentence to the *first*. You will be better able to see and hear whether each word group you read is a complete thought.

2   If you think a word group may be a fragment, ask yourself: Does this contain a subject and a verb and express a complete thought?

3   More specifically, be on the lookout for the most common fragments:

- Dependent-word fragments (starting with words like *after, because, since, when,* and *before*)

- *-ing* and *to* fragments (*-ing* and *to* at or near the start of a word group)

- Added-detail fragments (starting with words like *for example, such as, also,* and *especially*)

- Missing-subject fragments (a verb is present but not the subject)

▪ Review Test 1

Each word group in the following student paragraph is numbered. In the space provided, write C if a word group is a complete sentence; write F if it is a fragment. You will find eight fragments in the paragraph.

_____ 1. [1]I'm starting to think that there is no safe place left. [2]To ride a bicycle.

_____ 2. [3]When I try to ride on the highway, in order to go to school. [4]I feel like a

_____ 3. rabbit being pursued by predators. [5]Drivers whip past me at high speeds.

_____ 4. [6]And try to see how close they can get to my bike without actually killing

_____ 5. me. [7]When they pull onto the shoulder of the road or make a right turn.

_____ 6. [8]Drivers completely ignore my vehicle. [9]On city streets, I feel more like a

_____ 7. cockroach than a rabbit. [10]Drivers in the city despise bicycles. [11]Regardless of

_____ 8. an approaching bike rider. [12]Street-side car doors will unexpectedly open.

_____ 9. [13]Frustrated drivers who are stuck in traffic will make nasty comments. [14]Or

_____ 10. shout out obscene propositions. [15]Even pedestrians in the city show their

_____ 11. disregard for me. [16]While jaywalking across the street. [17]The pedestrian

_____ 12. will treat me, a law-abiding bicyclist, to a withering look of disdain.

_____ 13. [18]Pedestrians may even cross my path deliberately. [19]As if to prove their

_____ 14. higher position in the pecking order of the city streets. [20]Today, bicycling

_____ 15. can be hazardous to the rider's health.

_____ 16.

_____ 17.

_____ 18.

_____ 19.

_____ 20.

Now (on separate paper) correct the fragments you have found. Attach the fragments to sentences that come before or after them or make whatever other change is needed to turn each fragment into a sentence.

Handbook of Sentence Skills

▦ Review Test 2

Underline the two fragments in each item below. Then make whatever changes are needed to turn the fragments into sentences.

EXAMPLE Sharon was going to charge her new suit. But then decided to pay cash instead. She remembered her New Year's resolution. To cut down on her use of credit cards.

1. We both began to tire. As we passed the halfway mark in the race. But whenever I'd hear Reggie's footsteps behind me. I would pump my legs faster.

2. I have a few phobias. Such as fear of heights and fear of dogs. My nightmare is to be trapped in a hot-air balloon. With three German shepherds.

3. Punching all the buttons on his radio in sequence. Phil kept looking for a good song. He was in the mood to cruise down the highway. And sing at the top of his voice.

4. My children joke that we celebrate "Hanumas." With our Jewish neighbors. We share Hanukkah and Christmas activities. Including making potato pancakes at their house and decorating our tree.

5. I noticed two cartons of cigarettes. Sticking up out of my neighbor's trash bag. I realized he had made up his mind. To give up smoking for the fifth time this year.

6. I've decided to leave home. And rent an apartment. By being away from home and on my own. I will get along better with my parents.

7. The alley behind our house was flat. Except for a wide groove in the center. We used to sail paper boats down the groove. Whenever it rained hard enough to create a "river" there.

8. Don passed the computer school's aptitude test. Which qualifies him for nine months of training. Don kidded that anyone could be accepted. If he or she had $4,000.

■ **Review Test 3**

Turn each of the following word groups into a complete sentence.

EXAMPLES   With trembling hands

With trembling hands, I headed for the front of the classroom.

As the race wore on

Some runners dropped out as the race wore on.

1. After the storm passed

2. Such as fresh fruits and vegetables

3. During the mystery movie

4. Unless I study harder

5. Enrique, who works at his uncle's restaurant

6. Knocking over the table

7. To get to class on time

8. Hurrying to get dressed

9. Up in the attic

10. Losing my temper

26 Regular and Irregular Verbs

Regular Verbs

A Brief Review of Regular Verbs

18.1

Every verb has four principal parts: *present, past, past participle,* and *present participle.* These parts can be used to build all the verb *tenses*—the times shown by verbs.

Most verbs in English are regular. The past and past participle of a regular verb are formed by adding *-d* or *-ed* to the present. The *past participle* is the form of the verb used with the helping verbs *have, has,* or *had* (or some form of *be* with passive verbs). The *present participle* is formed by adding *-ing* to the present.

Here are the principal parts of some regular verbs:

Present	Past	Past Participle	Present Participle
shout	shouted	shouted	shouting
prepare	prepared	prepared	preparing
surprise	surprised	surprised	surprising
tease	teased	teased	teasing
frighten	frightened	frightened	frightening

Nonstandard Forms of Regular Verbs

Many people have grown up in communities where nonstandard forms of regular verbs are used in everyday speech. Instead of saying, for example, "That girl *looks* tired," a person using a community dialect might say, "That girl *look* tired." Instead of saying, "Yesterday I *fixed* the car," a person using a community dialect might say, "Yesterday I *fix* the car." Community dialects have richness and power but are a drawback in college and in the world of work, where regular English verb forms must be used.

Regular and Irregular Verbs

The following chart compares the nonstandard and the regular verb forms of the verb *work*.

Nonstandard Verb Form		Regular Verb Form	
(Do *not* use in your writing)		(Use for clear communication)	
Present tense			
I works	we works	I work	we work
you works	you works	you work	you work
he, she, it work	they works	he, she, it works	they work
Past tense			
I work	we work	I worked	we worked
you work	you work	you worked	you worked
he, she, it work	they work	he, she, it worked	they worked

To avoid nonstandard usage, memorize the forms shown above for the regular verb *work*. Then use the activities that follow to help make the inclusion of verb endings a writing habit.

Present Tense Endings   The verb ending -*s* or -*es* is needed with a regular verb in the present tense when the subject is *he, she, it,* or any *one person or thing.*

He reads every night.

She watches television every night.

It appears they have little in common.

ACTIVITY

Some verbs in the sentences that follow need -*s* or -*es* endings. Cross out each nonstandard verb form and write the standard form in the space provided.

_____   1. My radio wake me up every morning with soft music.

_____   2. Felix always clown around at the start of the class.

_____   3. My wife watch our baby in the morning, and I take over afternoons.

Handbook of Sentence Skills

_____ 4. Brenda want to go to nursing school next year.

_____ 5. My brain work much better at night than it does in early morning.

Past Tense Endings   The verb ending -d or -ed is needed with a regular verb in the past tense.

> This morning I completed my research paper.
> The recovering hospital patient walked slowly down the corridor.
> Some students hissed when the new assignment was given out.

ACTIVITY

Some verbs in the sentences that follow need -d or -ed endings. Cross out each nonstandard verb form and write the standard form in the space provided.

_____ 1. One of my teeth crack when I bit on the hard pretzel.

_____ 2. The accident victim complain of dizziness right before passing out.

_____ 3. We realize a package was missing when we got back from shopping.

_____ 4. I burn a hole in my shirt while ironing it.

_____ 5. The driver edge her car into the intersection while the light was still red.

Irregular Verbs

Irregular verbs have irregular forms in past tense and past participle. For example, the past tense of the irregular verb *choose* is *chose;* its past participle is *chosen.*

Almost everyone has some degree of trouble with irregular verbs. When you are unsure about the form of a verb, you can check the following list of irregular verbs. (The present participle is not shown on this list because it is formed simply by adding -ing to the base form of the verb.) Or you can check a dictionary, which gives the principal parts of irregular verbs.

A List of Irregular Verbs

Present	Past	Past Participle
arise	arose	arisen
awake	awoke *or* awaked	awoken *or* awaked
be (am, are, is)	was (were)	been

Regular and Irregular Verbs

Present	Past	Past Participle
become	became	become
begin	began	begun
bend	bent	bent
bite	bit	bitten
blow	blew	blown
break	broke	broken
bring	brought	brought
build	built	built
burst	burst	burst
buy	bought	bought
catch	caught	caught
choose	chose	chosen
come	came	come
cost	cost	cost
cut	cut	cut
do (does)	did	done
draw	drew	drawn
drink	drank	drunk
drive	drove	driven
eat	ate	eaten
fall	fell	fallen
feed	fed	fed
feel	felt	felt
fight	fought	fought
find	found	found
fly	flew	flown
freeze	froze	frozen
get	got	got *or* gotten
give	gave	given
go (goes)	went	gone
grow	grew	grown
have (has)	had	had
hear	heard	heard
hide	hid	hidden
hold	held	held
hurt	hurt	hurt
keep	kept	kept
know	knew	known
lay	laid	laid
lead	led	led

Handbook of Sentence Skills

Present	Past	Past Participle
leave	left	left
lend	lent	lent
let	let	let
lie	lay	lain
light	lit	lit
lose	lost	lost
make	made	made
meet	met	met
pay	paid	paid
ride	rode	ridden
ring	rang	rung
run	ran	run
say	said	said
see	saw	seen
sell	sold	sold
send	sent	sent
shake	shook	shaken
shrink	shrank	shrunk
shut	shut	shut
sing	sang	sung
sit	sat	sat
sleep	slept	slept
speak	spoke	spoken
spend	spent	spent
stand	stood	stood
steal	stole	stolen
stick	stuck	stuck
sting	stung	stung
swear	swore	sworn
swim	swam	swum
take	took	taken
teach	taught	taught
tear	tore	torn
tell	told	told
think	thought	thought
wake	woke *or* waked	woke *or* waked
wear	wore	worn
win	won	won
write	wrote	written

ACTIVITY

Cross out the incorrect verb form in each of the following sentences. Then write the correct form of the verb in the space provided.

_____flown_____ **EXAMPLE** After it had flew into the picture window, the dazed bird huddled on the ground.

_____ 1. As graduation neared, Michelle worried about the practicality of the major she'd chose.

_____ 2. Before we could find seats, the theater darkened and the opening credits begun to roll.

_____ 3. To be polite, I drunk the slightly sour wine that my grandfather poured from his carefully hoarded supply.

_____ 4. With a thunderous crack, the telephone pole breaked in half from the impact of the speeding car.

_____ 5. The inexperienced nurse shrunk from touching the patient's raw, burned skin.

_____ 6. After a day on the noisy construction site, Sam's ears rung for hours with a steady hum.

_____ 7. Sheila had forgot to write her social security number on the test form, so the computer rejected her answer sheet.

_____ 8. If I had went to work ten minutes earlier, I would have avoided being caught in the gigantic traffic snarl.

_____ 9. After the bicycle hit a patch of soft sand, the rider was throwed into the thorny bushes along the roadside.

_____ 10. Prehistoric people blowed paint over their outstretched hands to stencil their handprints on cave walls.

Nonstandard Forms of Three Common Irregular Verbs

People who use nonstandard forms of regular verbs also tend to use nonstandard forms of three common irregular verbs: *be, have,* and *do*. Instead of saying, for example, "My neighbors *are* nice people," a person using a nonstandard form might say, "My neighbors *be* nice people." Instead of saying, "She doesn't agree," they might say, "She *don't* agree." Instead of saying, "We have tickets," they might say, "We *has* tickets."

Handbook of Sentence Skills

The following charts compare the nonstandard and the standard forms of *be,* *have,* and *do.*

Be

	Community Dialect (Do *not* use in your writing)	Standard English (Use for clear communication)

Present tense

Community Dialect		Standard English	
~~I be~~ (*or* is)	we be	I am	we are
you be	you be	you are	you are
~~he, she,~~ it be	they be	he, she, it is	they are

Past tense

Community Dialect		Standard English	
I were	we was	I was	we were
you was	you was	you were	you were
he, she, it were	they was	he, she, it was	they were

Have

	Community Dialect (Do *not* use in your writing)	Standard English (Use for clear communication)

Present tense

Community Dialect		Standard English	
I has	we has	I have	we have
you has	you has	you have	you have
he, she, it have	they has	he, she, it has	they have

Past tense

Community Dialect		Standard English	
I has	we has	I had	we had
you has	you has	you had	you had
he, she, it have	they has	he, she, it had	they had

32

Regular and Irregular Verbs

Do

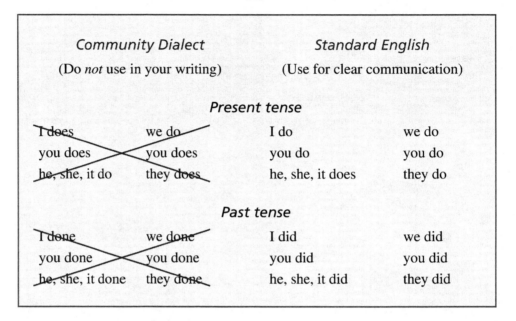

Community Dialect		Standard English	
(Do *not* use in your writing)		(Use for clear communication)	
Present tense			
~~I does~~	~~we do~~	I do	we do
you does	you does	you do	you do
~~he, she, it do~~	~~they does~~	he, she, it does	they do
Past tense			
~~I done~~	~~we done~~	I did	we did
you done	you done	you did	you did
~~he, she, it done~~	~~they done~~	he, she, it did	they did

Note   Many people have trouble with one negative form of *do*. They will say, for example, "He don't agree" instead of "He doesn't agree," or they will say "The door don't work" instead of "The door doesn't work." Be careful to avoid the common mistake of using *don't* instead of *doesn't*.

ACTIVITY

Cross out the nonstandard verb form in each sentence. Then write the standard form of *be, have,* or *do* in the space provided.

_____ 1. My cat, Tugger, be the toughest animal I know.

_____ 2. He have survived many close calls.

_____ 3. Three years ago, he were caught inside a car's engine.

_____ 4. He have one ear torn off and lost the sight in one eye.

_____ 5. We was surprised that he lived through the accident.

_____ 6. Within weeks, though, he were back to normal.

_____ 7. Then, last year, we was worried that we would lose Tugger.

_____ 8. Lumps that was growing on his back turned out to be cancer.

_____ 9. But the vet done an operation that saved Tugger's life.

_____ 10. By now, we know that Tugger really do have nine lives.

Handbook of Sentence Skills

■ Review Test 1

Cross out the incorrect verb form in each sentence. Then write the correct form in the space provided.

_____ 1. The health inspectors walk into the kitchen as the cook was picking up a hamburger off the floor.

_____ 2. The thieves would have stole my stereo, but I had had it engraved with a special identification number.

_____ 3. At the Chinese restaurant, Hollis choose his food by the number.

_____ 4. He had tore his girlfriend's picture into little pieces and tossed them out the window.

_____ 5. Because I has asthma, I carry an inhaler to use when I have trouble breathing.

_____ 6. Baked potatoes doesn't have as many calories as I thought.

_____ 7. The grizzly bear, with the dart dangling from its side, begun to feel the effects of the powerful tranquilizer.

_____ 8. Yesterday I check my bank balance and saw that my money was getting low.

_____ 9. Many childhood diseases has almost vanished in the United States.

_____ 10. Nancy sticked notes on the refrigerator with fruit-shaped magnets.

■ Review Test 2

Write short sentences that use the form requested for the following verbs.

EXAMPLE Past of *grow* ___*I grew my own tomatoes last year.*___

1. Past of *know* _____

2. Present of *take* _____

3. Past participle of *give* _____

4. Past participle of *write* _____

5. Past of *do* _____

6. Past of *talk* _____

7. Present of *begin* _____

8. Past of *go* _____

9. Past participle of *see* _____

10. Present of *drive* _____

25 Run-Ons

What Are Run-Ons?

A *run-on* is two complete thoughts that are run together with no adequate sign given to mark the break between them.*

Some run-ons have no punctuation at all to mark the break between the thoughts. Such run-ons are known as *fused sentences:* they are fused, or joined together, as if they were only one thought.

Fused Sentences

The bus stopped suddenly, I spilled coffee all over my shirt.

Mario told everyone in the room to be quiet his favorite show was on.

In other run-ons, known as *comma splices,* a comma is used to connect, or "splice" together, the two complete thoughts. However, a comma alone is *not enough* to connect two complete thoughts. Some stronger connection than a comma alone is needed.

Comma Splices

The bus stopped suddenly. I spilled coffee all over my shirt.

Mario told everyone in the room to be quiet, his favorite show was on.

Comma splices are the most common kind of run-on. Students sense that some kind of connection is needed between two thoughts, and so they often put a comma at the dividing point. But the comma alone is *not sufficient.* A stronger, clearer mark is needed between the two complete thoughts.

---

*Notes:

1. Some instructors regard all run-ons as fused sentences. But for many other instructors, and for our purposes in this book, the term *run-on* applies equally to fused sentences and comma splices. The bottom line is that you do not want either fused sentences or comma splices in your writing.

2. Some instructors refer to each complete thought in a run-on as an *independent clause. A clause* is simply a group of words having a subject and a verb. A clause may be *independent* (expressing a complete thought and able to stand alone) or *dependent* (not expressing a complete thought and not able to stand alone). Using this terminology, we'd say that a run-on is two independent clauses run together with no adequate sign given to mark the break between them.

Run-Ons

A Warning—Words That Can Lead to Run-Ons   People often write run-ons when the second complete thought begins with one of the following words:

I	we	there	now
you	they	this	then
he, she, it	that	next	

Whenever you use one of these words in writing a paper, remember to be on the alert for run-ons.

How to Correct Run-Ons

Here are three common methods of correcting a run-on:

1   Use a period and a capital letter to break the two complete thoughts into separate sentences:

The bus stopped suddenly. I spilled coffee all over my shirt.
Mario told everyone in the room to be quiet. His favorite show was on.

2   Use a comma plus a joining word (*and, but, for, or, nor, so, yet*) to connect the two complete thoughts:

The bus stopped suddenly, and I spilled coffee all over my shirt.
Mario told everyone in the room to be quiet, for his favorite show was on.

3   Use a semicolon to connect the two complete thoughts:

The bus stopped suddenly; I spilled coffee all over my shirt.
Mario told everyone in the room to be quiet; his favorite show was on.

A fourth method of correcting a run-on is to use *subordination*. The following activities will give you practice in the first three methods. Subordination is described fully on page 115, in the section of the book that deals with sentence variety.

Method 1: Period and a Capital Letter

One way of correcting a run-on is to use a period and a capital letter between the two complete thoughts. Use this method especially if the thoughts are not closely related or if another method would make the sentence too long.

ACTIVITY

In each of the following run-ons, locate the point at which one complete thought ends and another begins. Each is a *fused sentence*—that is, each consists of two sentences fused, or joined together, with no punctuation at all between them. Reading each sentence aloud will help you "hear" where a major break or split between the thoughts occurs. At such a point, your voice will probably drop and pause.

Correct the run-on by putting a period at the end of the first thought and a capital letter at the start of the next thought.

EXAMPLE   Bev's clock radio doesn't work anymore she spilled a glass of soda on it.

1. The men at the door claimed to have paving material left over from another job they wanted to pave our driveway for a "bargain price."

2. Linh, a paralegal who speaks Vietnamese, helps other people from her country write wills she assists others by going with them when they have to appear in court.

3. Vicky has her own unique style of dressing she wore a man's tuxedo with a red bow tie to her cousin's wedding.

4. In the summer, ants are attracted to water they will often enter a house through the dishwasher.

5. Humans have managed to adapt to any environment they can survive in Arctic wastes, tropical jungles, and barren deserts.

6. A five-year-old child knows over six thousand words he or she has also learned more than one thousand rules of grammar.

7. I rummaged around the crowded drawer looking for a pair of scissors then it suddenly stabbed me in the finger.

8. Squirrels like to jump from trees onto our roof their footsteps sound like ghosts running around our attic.

9. Today I didn't make good time driving to work every traffic light along the way was red.

10. Since I started using the Internet, I've sent hundreds of e-mails to my friends I never write letters by hand anymore.

Method 2: Comma and a Joining Word

Another way of correcting a run-on is to use a comma plus a joining word to connect the two complete thoughts. Joining words (also called *conjunctions*) include *and, but, for, or, nor, so,* and *yet.* Here is what the four most common joining words mean:

and   in addition

Teresa works full-time for an accounting firm, and she takes evening classes.

(*And* means *in addition:* Teresa works full-time for an accounting firm; *in addition,* she takes evening classes.)

but   however, on the other hand

I turned to the want ads, but I knew my dream job wouldn't be listed.

(*But* means *however:* I turned to the want ads; *however,* I knew my dream job wouldn't be listed.)

for   because

Lizards become sluggish at night, for they need the sun's warmth to maintain an active body temperature.

(*For* means *because:* Lizards become sluggish at night *because* they need the sun's warmth to maintain an active body temperature.)

so   as a result, therefore

    The canoe touched bottom, so Dave pushed it toward deeper water.

(*So* means *as a result:* The canoe touched bottom; *as a result,* Dave pushed it toward deeper water.)

ACTIVITY 1

Insert the joining word (*and, but, for, so*) that logically connects the two thoughts in each sentence.

1. Napoleon may have been a brave general, _____ he was afraid of cats.

2. The large dog was growling at me, _____ there were white bubbles of foam around its mouth.

3. The library had just closed, _____ I couldn't get any of the reserved books.

4. He checked on the new baby every five minutes, _____ he was afraid that something would happen to her.

5. Kate thought the milk was fresh, _____ it broke up into little sour flakes in her coffee.

6. Elephants have no thumbs, _____ baby elephants suck their trunks.

7. Lonnie heard a noise and looked out the window, _____ the only thing there was his reflection.

8. Although I like most creatures, I am not fond of snakes, _____ I like spiders even less.

9. My sister wants to exercise more and use her car less, _____ she walks to the grocery store.

10. Barry spends hours every day on his computer, _____ he often has the television on at the same time.

ACTIVITY 2

Add a complete and closely related thought to go with each of the following statements. Use a comma plus the indicated joining word when you write the second thought.

Run-Ons

EXAMPLE   for   I decided to leave school an hour early, _for I had a pounding_

headache.

but   1. The corner store is convenient _____

_____

for   2. Leo attended night class _____

_____

and   3. Aisha studied for an hour before dinner _____

_____

so   4. Paul can't retrieve his e-mail _____

_____

but   5. I needed a haircut _____

_____

ACTIVITY 3

Correct each run-on with either (1) a period and a capital letter or (2) a comma and a logical joining word. Do not use the same method of correction for every sentence.

Some of the run-ons are fused sentences (there is no punctuation between the two complete thoughts), and some are comma splices (there is only a comma between the two complete thoughts). One sentence is correct.

EXAMPLE   There was a strange odor in the house, Burt called the gas company ^so immediately.

1. Antonio got a can of soda from the refrigerator, then he walked outside to sit on the porch steps.

2. Cockroaches adapt to any environment they have even been found living inside nuclear reactors.

3. My dog was panting from the heat I decided to wet him down with the garden hose.

4. Our science class is working on a weather project with students from Russia we communicate by computer almost every day.

5. The best-selling items in the zoo gift shop are the stuffed pandas and the polar-bear T-shirts the profits from these items help support the real animals in the zoo.

6. The bristles of the paintbrushes were very stiff, soaking them in turpentine made them soft again.

7. Chen borrows cassettes from the library to listen to on the way to work, some are music, and some are recordings of best-selling books.

8. Last week, Rita's two boys chased the baby-sitter out of the house, now the sitter won't come back.

9. We knew a power failure had occurred, for all the clocks in the building were forty-seven minutes slow.

10. I volunteered to run the "Meals on Wheels" service in our city we deliver hot meals to sick or housebound people.

Method 3: Semicolon

A third method of correcting a run-on is to use a semicolon to mark the break between two thoughts. A *semicolon* (;) looks like a period above a comma and is sometimes called a *strong comma*. A semicolon signals more of a pause than a comma alone but not quite the full pause of a period. When it is used to correct run-ons, the semicolon can be used alone or with a transitional word.

Semicolon Alone   Here are some earlier sentences that were connected with a comma plus a joining word. Now they are connected by a semicolon alone. Notice that the semicolon alone—unlike the comma alone—can be used to connect the two complete thoughts in each sentence:

> Lonnie heard a noise and looked out the window; the only thing there was his reflection.
>
> He checked on the new baby every five minutes; he was afraid something would happen to her.
>
> Lizards become sluggish at night; they need the sun's warmth to maintain an active body temperature.

The large dog was growling at me; there were white bubbles of foam around its mouth.

We knew a power failure had occurred; all the clocks in the building were forty-seven minutes slow.

Using semicolons can add to sentence variety. For some people, however, the semicolon is a confusing punctuation mark. Keep in mind that if you are not comfortable using it, you can and should use one of the the first two methods of correcting run-ons.

ACTIVITY

Insert a semicolon where the break occurs between the two complete thoughts in each of the following sentences.

EXAMPLE   The plumber gave me an estimate of $60 I decided to repair the faucet myself.

1. The children stared at the artichokes on their plates they didn't know how to eat the strange vegetable.
2. I changed that lightbulb just last week now it's blown again.
3. The Great Wall of China is immense it's the only man-made structure visible from the Moon.
4. Elaine woke up at 3 A.M. to the smell of sizzling bacon her husband was having another insomnia attack.
5. Maya curled up under the covers she tried to get warm by grasping her icy feet with her chilly hands.
6. Three single mothers rent one house they share bills and help each other out.
7. Ice had formed on the inside edge of our window Joey scratched a J in it with his finger.
8. Charles peered into the microscope he saw only his own eyelashes.
9. A man in a bear suit walked slowly down the street the children stopped their play to stare at him.
10. I angrily punched a hole in the wall with my fist later I covered the hole with a picture.

Semicolon with a Transitional Word   A semicolon can be used with a transitional word and a comma to join two complete thoughts. Here are some examples:

Larry believes in being prepared for emergencies; therefore, he stockpiles canned goods in his basement.

I tried to cash my paycheck; however, I had forgotten to bring identification.

Athletic shoes must fit perfectly; otherwise, wearers may injure their feet or ankles.

A short nap at the end of the day relaxes me; in addition, it gives me the energy to spend the evening on my homework.

Some zoo animals have not learned how to be good parents; as a result, baby animals are sometimes brought up in zoo nurseries and even in private homes.

People use seventeen muscles when they smile; on the other hand, they use forty-three muscles when they frown.

Following is a list of common transitional words (also known as *adverbial conjunctions*), with brief meanings.

Transitional Word	Meaning
however	but
nevertheless	however
on the other hand	however
instead	as a substitute
meanwhile	in the intervening time
otherwise	under other conditions
indeed	in fact
in addition	also, and
also	in addition
moreover	in addition
furthermore	in addition
as a result	thus, therefore
thus	as a result
consequently	as a result
therefore	as a result

Run-Ons

ACTIVITY

For each sentence, choose a logical transitional word from the box above, and write it in the space provided. Use a semicolon *before* the connector and a comma *after* it.

EXAMPLE   I dread going to parties; _____*however,*_____ my husband loves meeting new people.

1. Jackie suffers from migraine headaches _____ her doctor has advised her to avoid caffeine and alcohol.

2. Ray's apartment is always neat and clean _____ the interior of his car looks like the aftermath of a tornado.

3. I try to attend all my math classes _____ I'll get too far behind to pass the weekly quizzes.

4. B. J. was singing Aretha Franklin tunes in the shower _____ his toast was burning in the kitchen.

5. The reporter was tough and experienced _____ even he was stunned by the tragic events.

A Note on Subordination

A fourth method of joining related thoughts is to use subordination. *Subordination* is a way of showing that one thought in a sentence is not as important as another thought. (Subordination is explained in full on page 115.) Below are three earlier sentences, recast so that one idea is subordinated to (made less important than) the other idea. In each case, the subordinate (or less important) thought is underlined. Note that each subordinate clause begins with a dependent word.

Because the library had just closed, I couldn't get any of the reserved books.

When the canoe touched bottom, Dave pushed the craft toward deeper water.

I didn't make good time driving to work today because every traffic light along the way was red.

Handbook of Sentence Skills

A Review: How to Check for Run-Ons

1 To see if a sentence is a run-on, read it aloud and listen for a break marking two complete thoughts. Your voice will probably drop and pause at the break.

2 To check an entire paper, read it aloud from the *last* sentence to the *first*. Doing so will help you hear and see each complete thought.

3 Be on the lookout for words that can lead to run-on sentences:

I	he, she, it	they	this	then	now
you	we	there	that	next	

4 Correct run-ons by using one of the following methods:

Period and a capital letter

Comma and a joining word (*and, but, for, or, nor, so, yet*)

Semicolon, alone or with a transitional word

Subordination

■ Review Test 1

Correct each run-on with either (1) a period and a capital letter or (2) a comma (if needed) and the joining word *and, but, for,* or *so.* Do not use the same method of correction for every sentence.

Some of the run-ons are fused sentences (there is no punctuation between the two complete thoughts), and some are comma splices (there is only a comma between the two complete thoughts). One sentence is correct.

1. Our boss expects us to work four hours without a break, he wanders off to a vending machine at least once an hour.

2. The children in the next car were making faces at other drivers, when I made a face back, they giggled and sank out of sight.

3. Chuck bent over and lifted the heavy tray then he heard an ominous crack in his back.

4. The branches of the tree were bare they made a dark feathery pattern against the orange-pink sunset.

5. In the dark alley, the air smelled like rotten garbage a large rat crept in the shadows.

6. Our class wanted to do something for the earthquake victims, we sent a donation to the Red Cross.

7. My ex-husband hit me just once in our marriage five minutes later I was packed and walking out the door.

8. Aunt Jeanne thought a warm dry climate would improve her health she moved to Arizona.

9. The average American teenager spends thirty-eight hours a week on schoolwork the average Japanese teenager spends about sixty.

10. We stocked our backpacks with high-calorie candy bars, and we also brought bags of dried apricots and peaches.

◼ Review Test 2

Correct each run-on by using (1) a period and a capital letter, (2) a comma and a joining word, or (3) a semicolon. Do not use one method exclusively.

1. The magazine had lain in the damp mailbox for two days its pages were blurry and swollen.

2. With a groan, Margo pried off her high heels, then she plunged her swollen feet into a bucket of baking soda and hot water.

3. At 2 A.M. the last customer left the diner, a busboy began stacking chairs on the tables for the night.

4. Hypnosis has nothing to do with the occult it is merely a state of deep relaxation.

5. Many young adults today live at home with their parents this allows them to save money.

6. I waited for the clanking train to clear the intersection rusty boxcars just kept rolling slowly along the rails.

7. Early in life, Thomas Edison suffered with deafness, he taught his wife- to-be Morse code while he was courting her.

8. Originally, horses were too small to carry riders very far larger horses had to be bred for use in warfare.

9. The words *month, silver, purple,* and *orange* have something in common, no other English words rhyme with them.

10. The broken soda machine dispensed a cup or soda, it would not provide both at the same time.

■ Review Test 3

Locate and correct the five run-ons in the passage that follows.

My worst experience of the week was going home for lunch, rather than eating at work. My children didn't know I was coming, they had used most of the bread. All I had to make a sandwich with were two thin, crumpled pieces of crust. I sat there eating my tattered sandwich and trying to relax, then the telephone rang. It was for my daughter, who was in the bathroom, she called down to me that I should get the person's name and number. As soon as I sat down again, someone knocked on the door, it was a neatly dressed couple with bright eyes who wanted to talk with me about a higher power in life. I politely got rid of them and went back to finish lunch. I thought I would relax over my coffee I had to break up a fight between my two young sons about which television channel to watch. As a last bit of frustration, my daughter came downstairs and asked me to drive her over to a friend's house before I went back to work.

■ Review Test 4

 On separate paper, write quickly for five minutes about what you did this past weekend. Don't worry about spelling, punctuation, finding exact words, or organizing your thoughts. Just focus on writing as many words as you can without stopping.

After you have finished, go back and correct any run-ons in your writing.

27 Subject-Verb Agreement

17

A verb must agree with its subject in number. A *singular subject* (one person or thing) takes a singular verb. A *plural subject* (more than one person or thing) takes a plural verb. Mistakes in subject-verb agreement are sometimes made in the following situations:

1   When words come between the subject and the verb
2   When a verb comes before the subject
3   With compound subjects
4   With indefinite pronouns

Each of these situations is explained in this chapter.

Words between Subject and Verb

Words that come between the subject and the verb do not change subject-verb agreement. In the sentence

The sharp <u>fangs</u> in the dog's mouth <u>look</u> scary.

the subject (*fangs*) is plural, and so the verb (*look*) is plural. The words that come between the subject and the verb are a prepositional phrase: *in the dog's mouth.* They do not affect subject-verb agreement. (A list of prepositions can be found on page 413.)

To help find the subject of certain sentences, you should cross out prepositional phrases.

17.5d

The lumpy <u>salt</u> ~~in the shakers~~ <u>needs</u> to be changed.
An old <u>chair</u> ~~with broken legs~~ <u>has sat</u> in our basement for years.

ACTIVITY

Underline the subject and lightly cross out any words that come between the subject and the verb. Then double-underline the verb in parentheses that you believe is correct.

1. Some members of the parents' association (want, wants) to ban certain books from the school library.
2. Chung's trench coat, with its big lapels and shoulder flaps, (make, makes) him feel like a tough private eye.
3. Misconceptions about apes like the gorilla (has, have) turned a relatively peaceful animal into a terrifying monster.
4. The rising cost of necessities like food and shelter (force, forces) many elderly people to live in poverty.
5. In my opinion, a few slices of pepperoni pizza (make, makes) a great evening.

Verb before Subject

A verb agrees with its subject even when the verb comes *before* the subject. Words that may precede the subject include *there, here,* and, in questions, *who, which, what,* and *where.*

Here are some examples of sentences in which the verb appears before the subject:

There are wild dogs in our neighborhood.

In the distance was a billow of black smoke.

Here is the newspaper.

Where are the children's coats?

If you are unsure about the subject, ask *who* or *what* of the verb. With the first example above, you might ask, "*What* are in our neighborhood?" The answer, *wild dogs,* is the subject.

ACTIVITY

Write the correct form of each verb in the space provided.

(is, are)   1. There _____ dozens of frenzied shoppers waiting for the store to open.

50

(is, are)   2. Here _____ the notes from yesterday's anthropology lecture.

(do, does)   3. When _____ we take our break?

(was, were)   4. There _____ scraps of yellowing paper stuck between the pages of the cookbook.

(was, were)   5. At the very bottom of the grocery list _____ an item that meant a trip all the way back to aisle one.

Compound Subjects

17.2

A *compound subject* is two subjects separated by a joining word, such as *and*. Subjects joined by *and* generally take a plural verb.

> A patchwork quilt and a sleeping bag cover my bed in the winter.
> Clark and Lois are a contented couple.

When subjects are joined by *either . . . or, neither . . . nor, not only . . . but also,* the verb agrees with the subject closer to the verb.

> Neither the negotiator nor the union leaders want the strike to continue.

The nearer subject, *leaders,* is plural, and so the verb is plural.

> Neither the union leaders nor the negotiator wants the strike to continue.

In this version, the nearer subject, *negotiator,* is singular, so the verb is singular.

ACTIVITY

Write the correct form of the verb in the space provided.

(sit, sits)   1. A crusty baking pan and a greasy plate _____ on the countertop.

(cover, covers)   2. Spidery cracks and a layer of dust _____ the ivory keys on the old piano.

(know, knows)   3. Not only the assistant managers but also the secretary _____ that the company is folding.

(was, were)   4. In eighteenth-century France, makeup and high heels _____ worn by men.

(smell, smells)   5. Either the trash can or those socks _____ horrible.

Indefinite Pronouns

17.5

The following words, known as *indefinite pronouns,* always take singular verbs:

(-one words)	*(-body* words)	*(-thing* words)	
one	nobody	nothing	each
anyone	anybody	anything	either
everyone	everybody	everything	neither
someone	somebody	something	

Note   *Both* always takes a plural verb.

ACTIVITY

Write the correct form of the verb in the space provided.

(suit, suits)   1. Neither of those hairstyles _____ the shape of your face.

(mention, mentions)   2. Somebody without much sensitivity always _____ my birthmark.

(is, are)   3. Both of the puppies _____ cute in their own ways.

(enter, enters)   4. Everyone _____ the college kite-flying contest in the spring.

(fall, falls)   5. One of these earrings constantly _____ off my ear.

■ Review Test 1

In the space provided, write the correct form of the verb shown in the margin.

(is, are)   1. Some wheelchair-bound patients, as a result of a successful experiment, _____ using trained monkeys as helpers.

(was, were)   2. Each of their children _____ given a name picked at random from a page of the Bible.

(seem, seems)   3. Many of the headlines in the *National Enquirer* _____ hard to believe.

(is, are)   4. Envelopes, file folders, and a telephone book _____ jammed into Lupe's kitchen drawers.

(contains, contain)   5. Neither of the main dishes at tonight's dinner _____ any meat.

(damage, damages)   6. The use of metal chains and studded tires _____ roadways because metal and studs chip away at the paved surface.

(was, were)   7. Next to the cash register _____ a can for donations to the animal protection society.

(makes, make)   8. A metal grab bar bolted onto the tiles _____ it easier for elderly people to get into and out of the bathtub.

(cleans, clean)   9. In exchange for reduced rent, Karla and James _____ the dentist's office beneath their second-floor apartment.

(is, are)   10. One of the hospital's delivery rooms _____ furnished with bright carpets and curtains to resemble a room at home.

■ Review Test 2

Cross out the incorrect verb form in each sentence. In addition, underline the subject or subjects that go with the verb. Then write the correct form of the verb in the space provided.

_____ 1. Why is Martha and her mother digging a hole in their garden so late at night?

_____ 2. Neither of my children look like me.

_____ 3. Three goats, a potbellied pig, and a duck was among the entrants in the pet parade.

_____ 4. The little balls all over my pink sweater looks like woolen goose bumps.

_____ 5. Here is the low-calorie cola and the double-chocolate cake you ordered.

_____ 6. The odor of those perfumed ads interfere with my enjoyment of a magazine.

_____ 7. One of my roommates are always leaving wet towels on the bathroom floor.

_____ 8. A tiny piece of gum and some tape is holding my old glasses together.

_____ 9. A person in his or her forties often begin to think about making a contribution to the world and not just about himself or herself.

_____ 10. Each of the child's thirty-four stuffed animals have a name and an entire life history.

Handbook of Sentence Skills

■ Review Test 3

Complete each of the following sentences using *is, are, was, were, have,* or *has.* Then underline the subject.

EXAMPLE For me, <u>popcorn</u> at the movies *is like coffee at breakfast.*

1. The <u>magazines</u> under my roommate's bed _____

2. The <u>car</u> with the purple fenders _____

3. My <u>boss</u> and her secretary _____

4. Neither of the football players _____

5. Here _____

28 Additional Information about Verbs

The purpose of this chapter is to provide additional information about verbs. Some people will find the grammatical terms here a helpful reminder of what they've learned earlier, in school, about verbs. For them, the terms will increase their understanding of how verbs function in English. Other people may welcome more detailed information about terms used elsewhere in the text. In either case, remember that the most common mistakes people make with verbs have been treated in previous chapters of the book.

Verb Tense

18.1

Verbs tell us the time of an action. The time that a verb shows is usually called *tense*. The most common tenses are the simple present, past, and future. In addition, there are nine tenses that enable us to express more specific ideas about time than we could with the simple tenses alone. Following are the twelve verb tenses and examples of each tense. Read them over to increase your sense of the many different ways of expressing time in English.

Tenses	Examples
Present	I *work.* Tony *works.*
Past	Ellen *worked* on her car.
Future	You *will work* on a new project next week.
Present perfect	He *has worked* on his term paper for a month. They *have worked* out a compromise.
Past perfect	The nurse *had worked* two straight shifts.
Future perfect	Next Monday, I *will have worked* here exactly two years.

continued

Handbook of Sentence Skills

Tenses	Examples
Present progressive	I *am working* on my speech for the debate. You *are working* too hard. The tape recorder *is* not *working* properly.
Past progressive	He *was working* in the basement. The contestants *were working* on their talent routines.
Future progressive	My son *will be working* in our store this summer.
Present perfect progressive	Sarah *has been working* late this week.
Past perfect progressive	Until recently, I *had been working* nights.
Future perfect progressive	My mother *will have been working* as a nurse for forty-five years by the time she retires.

ACTIVITY

On a separate paper, write twelve sentences using the twelve verb tenses.

Helping Verbs

18.3

There are three common verbs that can either stand alone or combine with (and "help") other verbs. Here are the verbs and their forms:

> be (am, are, is, was, were, being, been)
> have (has, having, had)
> do (does, did)

Here are examples of the helping verbs:

Additional Information about Verbs

Used Alone	**Used as Helping Verbs**
I *was* angry.	I *was growing* angry.
Sue *has* the key.	Sue *has forgotten* the key.
He *did* well in the test.	He *did fail* the previous test.

There are nine helping verbs (traditionally known as *modals,* or *modal auxiliaries*) that are always used in combination with other verbs. Here are the nine verbs and a sentence example of each:

can	I *can see* the rainbow.
could	I *could* not *find* a seat.
may	The game *may be postponed.*
might	Cindy *might resent* your advice.
shall	I *shall see* you tomorrow.
should	He *should get* his car serviced.
will	Tony *will want* to see you.
would	They *would* not *understand.*
must	You *must visit* us again.

Note from the examples that these verbs have only one form. They do not, for instance, add an *-s* when used with *he, she, it,* or any one person or thing.

ACTIVITY

On separate paper, write nine sentences using the nine helping verbs.

Verbals

18.4

Verbals are words formed from verbs. Verbals, like verbs, often express action. They can add variety to your sentences and vigor to your writing style. The three kinds of verbals are *infinitives, participles,* and *gerunds.*

Infinitive

An infinitive is *to* plus the base form of the verb.

> I love *to dance*.
>
> Lina hopes *to write* for a newspaper.
>
> I asked the children *to clean* the kitchen.

Participle

A participle is a verb form used as an adjective (a descriptive word). The present participle ends in *-ing*. The part participle ends in *-ed* or has an irregular ending.

> *Peering* into the cracked mirror, the *crying* woman wiped her eyes.
>
> The *astounded* man stared at his *winning* lottery ticket.
>
> *Swinging* a sharp ax, Omar split the *rotted* beam.

Gerund

A gerund is the *-ing* form of a verb used as a noun.

> *Swimming* is the perfect exercise.
>
> *Eating* junk food is my diet downfall.
>
> Through *doodling,* people express their inner feelings.

ACTIVITY

On separate paper, write three sentences using infinitives, three sentences using participles, and three sentences using gerunds.

29 Pronoun Agreement and Reference

Nouns name persons, places, or things. *Pronouns* are words that take the place of nouns. In fact, the word *pronoun* means "for a noun." Pronouns are shortcuts that keep you from unnecessarily repeating words in writing. Here are some examples of pronouns:

> Eddie left *his* camera on the bus.
> (*His* is a pronoun that takes the place of *Eddie's*.)
>
> Elena drank the coffee even though *it* was cold.
> (*It* replaces *coffee*.)
>
> As I turned the newspaper's damp pages, *they* disintegrated in my hands.
> (*They* is a pronoun that takes the place of *pages*.)

This chapter presents rules that will help you avoid two common mistakes people make with pronouns. The rules are:

1   A pronoun must agree in number with the word or words it replaces.

2   A pronoun must refer clearly to the word it replaces.

Pronoun Agreement

17.8

A pronoun must agree in number with the word or words it replaces. If the word a pronoun refers to is singular, the pronoun must be singular; if that word is plural, the pronoun must be plural. (Note that the word a pronoun refers to is known as the *antecedent*.)

> Marie showed me *her* antique wedding band.

> Students enrolled in the art class must provide *their* own supplies.

In the first example, the pronoun *her* refers to the singular word *Marie;* in the second example, the pronoun *their* refers to the plural word *Students.*

Handbook of Sentence Skills

ACTIVITY

Write the appropriate pronoun (*their, they, them, it*) in the blank space in each of the following sentences.

EXAMPLE   I opened the wet umbrella and put ___*it*___ in the bathtub to dry.

1. Kate and Omar left for the movies earlier than usual, because _____ knew the theater would be packed.

2. The clothes were still damp, but I decided to fold _____ anyway.

3. Young adults often face a difficult transition period when _____ leave home for the first time.

4. Paul's grandparents renewed _____ marriage vows at a huge fiftieth wedding anniversary celebration.

5. The car's steering wheel began to pull to one side, and then _____ started to shimmy.

Indefinite Pronouns

17.8

The following words, known as *indefinite pronouns,* are always singular.

(-*one* words)	(-*body* words)	
one	nobody	each
anyone	anybody	either
everyone	everybody	neither
someone	somebody	

If a pronoun in a sentence refers to one of these singular words, the pronoun should be singular.

Somebody left her shoulder bag on the back of a chair.

One of the busboys just called and said he would be an hour late.

Everyone in the club must pay his dues next week.

Each circled pronoun is singular because it refers to an indefinite pronoun.

Pronoun Agreement and Reference

Note   There are two important points to remember about indefinite pronouns:

1   In the last example, if everyone in the club was a woman, the pronoun would be *her.* If the club had women and men, the pronoun would be *his or her:*

> Everyone in the club must pay his or her dues next week.

Some writers follow the traditional practice of using *his* to refer to both women and men. Some now use *his or her* to avoid an implied sexual bias. To avoid using *his* or the somewhat awkward *his or her,* a sentence can often be rewritten in the plural:

> Club members must pay their dues next week.

2   In informal spoken English, *plural* pronouns are often used with the indefinite pronouns. Many people would probably not say:

> Everybody has his or her own opinion about the election.

Instead, they would be likely to say:

> Everybody has their own opinion about the election.

Here are other examples:

> Everyone in the choir must buy their robes.
> Everybody in the line has their ticket ready.
> No one in the class remembered to bring their books.

In such cases, the indefinite pronouns are clearly plural in meaning, and using them helps people avoid the awkward *his or her.* In time, the plural pronoun may be accepted in formal speech or writing. Until then, however, you should use the grammatically correct singular form in your writing.

ACTIVITY

Underline the correct pronoun.

1. Neither of the potential buyers had really made up (her, their) mind.
2. Not one of the new cashiers knows what (he, they) should be doing.
3. Each of these computers has (its, their) drawbacks.

Handbook of Sentence Skills

4. Anyone trying to reduce (his or her, their) salt intake should avoid canned and processed foods.

5. If anybody calls when I'm out, tell (him, them) I'll return in an hour.

Pronoun Reference

19.5

A sentence may be confusing and unclear if a pronoun appears to refer to more than one word or does not refer to any specific word. Look at this sentence:

Miriam was annoyed when they failed her car for a faulty turn signal.

Who failed her car? There is no specific word that *they* refers to. Be clear:

Miriam was annoyed when the inspectors failed her car for a faulty turn signal.

Here are sentences with other faulty pronoun references. Read the explanations of why they are faulty and look carefully at how they are corrected.

Faulty	**Clear**
Peter told Alan that his wife was unhappy. (Whose wife is unhappy: Peter's or Alan's? Be clear.)	Peter told Alan, "My wife is unhappy."
Kia is really a shy person, but she keeps it hidden. (There is no specific word that *it* refers to. It would not make sense to say, "Kia keeps shy hidden.")	Kia is really a shy person, but she keeps her shyness hidden.
Marsha attributed her success to her husband's support, which was generous. (Does *which* mean that Marsha's action was generous or that her husband's support was generous?)	Generously, Marsha attributed her success to her husband's support. *Or:* Marsha attributed her success to her husband's generous support.

ACTIVITY

Rewrite each of the following sentences to make clear the vague pronoun reference. Add, change, or omit words as necessary.

62

Pronoun Agreement and Reference

EXAMPLE Susan's mother wondered if she was tall enough to be a model.

_____

1. Dad spent all day fishing but didn't catch a single one.

_____

2. At that fast-food restaurant, they give you free glasses with your soft drinks.

_____

3. Ruth told Denise that her bouts of depression were becoming serious.

_____

4. Dipping her spoon into the pot of simmering spaghetti sauce, Helen felt it slip out of her hand.

_____

5. Pete visited the tutoring center because they can help him with his economics course.

_____

■ Review Test 1

Underline the correct word in parentheses.

1. Each of the little girls may choose one prize for (her, their) own.
2. I asked at the body shop how quickly (they, the shop employees) could fix my car.
3. The coaches told each member of the football team that (his, their) position was the most important in the game.
4. Darlene tried to take notes during the class, but she didn't really understand (it, the subject).
5. When someone has a cold, (they, he or she) should take extra vitamin C and drink a lot of fluids.

■ Review Test 2

Cross out the pronoun error in each of the following sentences, and write the correction in the space provided at the left. Then circle the letter that correctly describes the type of error that was made.

Handbook of Sentence Skills

EXAMPLES

his (or her) Anyone without a ticket will lose their place in the line.
Mistake in a. pronoun reference (b.) pronoun agreement

Ellen (or Kim) When Ellen takes her daughter Kim to the park, she enjoys herself.
Mistake in (a.) pronoun reference b. pronoun agreement

_____ 1. Could someone volunteer their services to clean up after the party?
Mistake in a. pronoun reference b. pronoun agreement

_____ 2. The referee watched the basketball game closely to make sure they didn't commit any fouls.
Mistake in a. pronoun reference b. pronoun agreement

_____ 3. If job-hunters want to make a good impression at an interview, he should be sure to arrive on time.
Mistake in a. pronoun reference b. pronoun agreement

_____ 4. Neither of those girls appreciates their parents' sacrifices.
Mistake in a. pronoun reference b. pronoun agreement

_____ 5. There wasn't much to do on Friday nights after they closed the only movie theater in town.
Mistake in a. pronoun reference b. pronoun agreement

30 Pronoun Types

This chapter describes some common types of pronouns: subject and object pronouns, possessive pronouns, and demonstrative pronouns.

Subject and Object Pronouns

 19.2

Most pronouns change their form depending on what place they occupy in a sentence. In the box that follows is a list of subject and object pronouns.

Subject Pronouns	Object Pronouns
I	me
you	you (no change)
he	him
she	her
it	it (no change)
we	us
they	them

Subject Pronouns

Subject pronouns are subjects of verbs.

> *He* served as a soldier during the war in Iraq. (*He* is the subject of the verb *served*.)

> *They* are moving into our old apartment. (*They* is the subject of the verb *are moving*.)

> *We* students should have a say in the decision. (*We* is the subject of the verb *should have*.)

Handbook of Sentence Skills

Following are several rules for using subject pronouns—and several kinds of mistakes people sometimes make with subject pronouns.

Rule 1   Use a subject pronoun when you have a compound subject (more than one subject).

Incorrect	Correct
My brother and *me* are Bruce Springsteen fanatics.	My brother and *I* are Bruce Springsteen fanatics.
Him and *me* know the lyrics to all of Bruce's songs.	*He* and *I* know the lyrics to all of Bruce's songs.

Hint for Rule 1   If you are not sure what pronoun to use, try each pronoun by itself in the sentence. The correct pronoun will be the one that sounds right. For example, "Him knows the lyrics to all of Bruce's songs" does not sound right; "He knows the lyrics to all of Bruce's songs" does.

Rule 2   Use a subject pronoun after forms of the verb *be*. Forms of *be* include *am, are, is, was, were, has been, have been,* and others.

It was *I* who left the light on.

It may be *they* in that car.

It is *he.*

The sentences above may sound strange and stilted to you because they are seldom used in conversation. When we speak with one another, forms such as "It was me," "It may be them," and "It is him" are widely accepted. In formal writing, however, the grammatically correct forms are still preferred.

Hint for Rule 2   You can avoid having to use a subject pronoun after *be* by simply rewording a sentence. Here is how the preceding examples could be reworded:

I was the one who left the light on.

They may be in that car.

He is here.

Pronoun Types

Rule 3   Use subject pronouns after *than* or *as*. The subject pronoun is used because a verb is understood after the pronoun.

> You play better than I (play). (The verb *play* is understood after *I*.)
>
> Jenny is as bored as I (am). (The verb *am* is understood after *I*.)
>
> We don't need the money as much as they (do). (The verb *do* is understood after *they*.)

Hint for Rule 3   Avoid mistakes by mentally adding the "missing" verb at the end of the sentence.

Object Pronouns

Object pronouns (*me, him, her, us, them*) are the objects of verbs or prepositions. (*Prepositions* are connecting words like *for, at, about, to, before, by, with*, and *of*. See also page 413.)

> Tony helped me. (*Me* is the object of the verb *helped*.)
>
> We took *them* to the college. (*Them* is the object of the verb *took*.)
>
> Leave the children with *us*. (*Us* is the object of the preposition *with*.)
>
> I got in line behind *him*. (*Him* is the object of the preposition *behind*.)

People are sometimes uncertain about what pronoun to use when two objects follow a verb.

Incorrect	**Correct**
I gave a gift to Ray and *she*.	I gave a gift to Ray and *her*.
She came to the movie with Bobbie and *I*.	She came to the movie with Bobbie and *me*.

Hint   If you are not sure what pronoun to use, try each pronoun by itself in the sentence. The correct pronoun will be the one that sounds right. For example, "I gave a gift to she" does not sound right; "I gave a gift to her" does.

ACTIVITY

Underline the correct subject or object pronoun in each of the following sentences. Then show whether your answer is a subject or object pronoun by circling the S or O in the margin. The first one is done for you as an example.

Handbook of Sentence Skills

S Ⓞ   1. The sweaters Mom knitted for Victor and (I, me) are too small.

S O   2. The umpire and (he, him) started to argue.

S O   3. No one has a quicker temper than (she, her).

S O   4. Your grades prove that you worked harder than (they, them).

S O   5. (We, Us) runners train indoors when the weather turns cold.

S O   6. (She, Her) and Betty never put the cap back on the toothpaste.

S O   7. Chris and (he, him) are the most energetic kids in the first grade.

S O   8. Arguing over clothes is a favorite pastime for my sister and (I, me).

S O   9. The rest of (they, them) will be arriving in about ten minutes.

S O   10. The head of the ticket committee asked Melba and (I, me) to help with sales.

Possessive Pronouns

19.2c

Here is a list of possessive pronouns:

my, mine	our, ours
your, yours	your, yours
his	their, theirs
her, hers	
its	

Possessive pronouns show ownership or possession.

Adam revved up *his* motorcycle and blasted off.
The keys are *mine*.

Note   A possessive pronoun *never* uses an apostrophe. (See also page 504.)

Incorrect

That coat is *hers'*.
The card table is *theirs'*.

Correct

That coat is *hers*.
The card table is *theirs*.

68

Pronoun Types

ACTIVITY

Cross out the incorrect pronoun form in each of the sentences below. Write the correct form in the space at the left.

EXAMPLE ___*hers*___ Those gloves are hers'.

_____ 1. I discovered that my car had somehow lost its' rear license plate.

_____ 2. Are those seats theirs'?

_____ 3. I knew that sweater was hers' when I saw the monogram.

_____ 4. The dog in that cage is our's.

_____ 5. These books are yours' if you want them.

Demonstrative Pronouns

Demonstrative pronouns point to or single out a person or thing. There are four demonstrative pronouns:

this	these
that	those

Generally speaking, *this* and *these* refer to things close at hand; *that* and *those* refer to things farther away. The four demonstrative pronouns are also commonly used as demonstrative adjectives.

Is anyone using *this* spoon?

I am going to throw away *these* magazines.

I just bought *that* black pickup truck at the curb.

Pick up *those* toys in the corner.

Note   Do not use *them, this here, that there, these here,* or *those there* to point out. Use only *this, that, these,* or *those.*

Handbook of Sentence Skills

ACTIVITY

Cross out the incorrect form of the demonstrative pronoun, and write the correct form in the space provided.

EXAMPLE ___*Those*___ ~~Them~~ tires look worn.

_____ 1. This here map is out of date.

_____ 2. Leave them keys out on the coffee table.

_____ 3. I've seen them girls somewhere before.

_____ 4. Jack entered that there dog in an obedience contest.

_____ 5. Where are them new knives?

■ Review Test

Underline the correct word in the parentheses.

1. If the contract negotiations are left up to (they, them), we'll have to accept the results.
2. (Them, Those) student crafts projects have won several awards.
3. Our grandmother told David and (I, me) to leave our muddy shoes outside on the porch.
4. The judge decided that the fault was (theirs', theirs) and ordered them to pay the damages.
5. I gave the money to (she, her) and asked her to put it in the bank's night deposit slot.
6. The black-masked raccoon stared at Rudy and (I, me) for an instant and then ran away.
7. When we saw the smashed window, Lynn and (I, me) didn't know whether to enter the house.
8. (This here, This) is my cousin Manuel.
9. This coat can't be (hers, her's); it's too small.
10. Because we weren't wearing shoes, Tara and (I, me) had a hard time walking on the sharp gravel.

31 Adjectives and Adverbs

Adjectives

What Are Adjectives?

Adjectives describe nouns (names of persons, places, or things) or pronouns.

> Yoko is a *wise* woman. (The adjective *wise* describes the noun *woman*.)
>
> She is also *funny*. (The adjective *funny* describes the pronoun *she*.)
>
> I'll carry the *heavy* bag of groceries. (The adjective *heavy* describes the noun *bag*.)
>
> It is *torn*. (The adjective *torn* describes the pronoun *it*.)

Adjectives usually come before the word they describe (as in *wise* woman and *heavy* bag). But they also come after forms of the verb *be* (*is, are, was, were,* and so on). They also follow verbs such as *look, appear, seem, become, sound, taste,* and *smell.*

> That road is *slippery*. (The adjective *slippery* describes the road.)
>
> The dogs are *noisy*. (The adjective *noisy* describes the dogs.)
>
> Those customers were *impatient*. (The adjective *impatient* describes the customers.)
>
> Your room looks *neat*. (The adjective *neat* describes the room.)

Using Adjectives to Compare

For all one-syllable adjectives and some two-syllable adjectives, add *-er* when comparing two things and *-est* when comparing three or more things.

> Phil's beard is *longer* than mine, but Lee's is the *longest*.
>
> Meg may be the *quieter* of the two sisters; but that's not saying much, since they're the *loudest* girls in school.

Handbook of Sentence Skills

For some two-syllable adjectives and all longer adjectives, use *more* when comparing two things and *most* when comparing three or more things.

> Liza Minnelli is *more famous* than her sister; but their mother, Judy Garland, is still the *most famous* member of the family.

> The red letters on the sign are *more noticeable* than the black ones, but the Day-Glo letters are the *most noticeable.*

You can usually tell when to use *more* and *most* by the sound of a word. For example, you can probably tell by its sound that "carefuller" would be too awkward to say and that *more careful* is thus correct. But there are many words for which both *-er* or *-est* and *more* or *most* are equally correct. For instance, either "a more fair rule" or "a fairer rule" is correct.

To form negative comparisons, use *less* and *least.*

> During my first dance class, I felt *less graceful* than an injured elephant.

> When the teacher came to our house to complain to my parents, I offered her the *least* comfortable chair in the room.

Points to Remember about Comparing

Point 1   Use only one form of comparison at a time. That is, do not use both an *-er* ending and *more* or both an *-est* ending and *most:*

Incorrect	Correct
My mother's suitcase is always *more heavier* than my father's.	My mother's suitcase is always *heavier* than my father's.
Psycho is still the *most frighteningest* movie I've ever seen	*Psycho* is still the *most frightening* movie I've ever seen.

Point 2   Learn the irregular forms of the words shown below.

	Comparative (for comparing two things)	Superlative (for comparing three or more things)
bad	worse	worst
good, well	better	best
little (in amount)	less	least
much, many	more	most

Adjectives and Adverbs

Do not use both *more* and an irregular comparative or *most* and an irregular superlative.

Incorrect	**Correct**
It is *more better* to give than to receive.	It is *better* to give than to receive.
Last night I got the *most worst* snack attack I ever had.	Last night I got the *worst* snack attack I ever had.

ACTIVITY

Add to each sentence the correct form of the word in the margin.

bad   **EXAMPLES** The _____*worst*_____ job I ever had was baby-sitting for spoiled four-year-old twins.

wonderful   The ___*most wonderful*___ day of my life was when my child was born.

good   1. The _____ chocolate cake I ever ate had bananas in it.

young   2. Aunt Sonja is the _____ of the three sisters.

bad   3. A rain that freezes is _____ than a snowstorm.

unusual   4. That's the _____ home I've ever seen—it's shaped like a teapot.

little   5. Being painfully shy has made Leon the _____ friendly person I know.

Adverbs

What Are Adverbs?

20.6

Adverbs describe verbs, adjectives, or other adverbs. They usually end in *-ly*.

The father *gently* hugged the sick child. (The adverb *gently* describes the verb *hugged*.)

Newborns are *totally* innocent. (The adverb *totally* describes the adjective *innocent*.)

The lecturer spoke so *terribly* fast that I had trouble taking notes. (The adverb *terribly* describes the adverb *fast*.)

A Common Mistake with Adverbs and Adjectives

People often mistakenly use an adjective instead of an adverb after a verb.

Incorrect	Correct
Sam needs a haircut *bad.*	Sam needs a haircut *badly.*
I laugh too *loud* when I'm embarrassed.	I laugh too *loudly* when I'm embarrassed.
You might have won the race if you hadn't run so *slow* at the beginning.	You might have won the race if you hadn't run so *slowly* at the beginning.

ACTIVITY

Underline the adjective or adverb needed. (Remember that adjectives describe nouns, and adverbs describe verbs and other adverbs.)

1. As Mac danced, his earring bounced (rapid, rapidly).
2. A drop of (thick, thickly) pea soup dripped down his chin.
3. I hiccuped (continuous, continuously) for fifteen minutes.
4. The detective opened the door (careful, carefully).
5. All she heard when she answered the phone was (heavy, heavily) breathing.

Well and *Good*

Two words that are often confused are *well* and *good*. *Good* is an adjective; it describes nouns. *Well* is usually an adverb; it describes verbs. But *well* (rather than *good*) is used as an adjective when referring to health.

ACTIVITY

Write *well* or *good* in each of the sentences that follow.

1. If you kids do a _____ job of cleaning the garage, I'll take you out for some ice cream.

2. If I organize the office records too _____, my bosses may not need me anymore.

3. After eating a pound of peanuts, I didn't feel too _____.

74

4. When Ernie got AIDS, he discovered who his _____ friends really were.

5. Just because brothers and sisters fight when they're young doesn't mean they won't get along _____ as adults.

■ Review Test 1

Underline the correct word in parentheses.

1. The waitress poured (littler, less) coffee into my cup than yours.
2. Humid air seems to make Sid's asthma (more worse, worse).
3. The movie is so interesting that the three hours pass (quick, quickly).
4. The talented boy sang as (confident, confidently) as a seasoned performer.
5. Our band played so (good, well) that a local firm hired us for its annual dinner.
6. Tamika is always (truthful, truthfully), even when it might be better to tell a white lie.
7. The driver stopped the bus (sudden, suddenly) and yelled, "Everybody out!"
8. Shirt and pants in the same color make you look (more thin, thinner) than ones in contrasting colors.
9. Your intentions may have been (good, well), but I'd prefer that you ask before arranging a blind date for me.
10. Our cat likes to sit in the (warmest, most warm) spot in any room—by a fireplace, on a windowsill in the sunshine, or on my lap.

■ Review Test 2

Write a sentence that uses each of the following adjectives and adverbs correctly.

1. careless _____

2. angrily _____

3. well _____

4. most relaxing _____

5. best _____

32 Misplaced Modifiers

16.2

Misplaced modifiers are words that, because of awkward placement, do not describe what the writer intended them to describe. A misplaced modifier can make a sentence confusing or unintentionally funny. To avoid this, place words as close as possible to what they describe.

Misplaced Words	**Correctly Placed Words**
George couldn't drive to work in his small sports car *with a broken leg.* (The sports car had a broken leg?)	With a broken leg, George couldn't drive to work in his small sports car. (The words describing George are now placed next to *George.*)
The toaster was sold to us by a charming salesman *with a money-back guarantee.* (The salesman had a money-back guarantee?)	The toaster with a money-back guarantee was sold to us by a charming salesman. (The words describing the toaster are now placed next to it.)
He *nearly* brushed his teeth for twenty minutes every night. (He came close to brushing his teeth but in fact did not brush them at all?)	He brushed his teeth for nearly twenty minutes every night. (The meaning—that he brushed his teeth for a long time—is now clear.)

ACTIVITY

Underline the misplaced word or words in each sentence. Then rewrite the sentence, placing related words together and thereby making the meaning clear.

EXAMPLES   Frozen shrimp lay in the steel pans that were thawing rapidly.

Frozen shrimp that were thawing rapidly lay in the steel pans.

The speaker discussed the problem of crowded prisons at the college.

At the college, the speaker discussed the problem of crowded prisons.

Misplaced Modifiers

1. The patient talked about his childhood on the psychiatrist's couch.

   _____

2. The crowd watched the tennis players with swiveling heads.

   _____

3. Vonnie put four hamburger patties on the counter which she was cooking for dinner.

   _____

4. Steve carefully hung the new suit that he would wear to his first job interview in the bedroom closet.

   _____

5. Anne ripped the shirt on a car door that she made in sewing class.

   _____

6. The latest Denzel Washington movie has almost opened in 2,200 theaters across the country.

   _____

7. The newscaster spoke softly into a microphone wearing a bulletproof vest.

   _____

8. The tenants left town in a dilapidated old car owing two months' rent.

   _____

9. The woman picked up a heavy frying pan with arthritis.

   _____

10. I discovered an unusual plant in the greenhouse that oozed a milky juice.

    _____

Review Test 1

Write MM for *misplaced modifier* or C for *correct* in the space provided for each sentence.

_____ 1. I nearly napped for twenty minutes during the biology lecture.

_____ 2. I napped for nearly twenty minutes during the biology lecture.

_____ 3. Ron paused as the girl he had been following stopped at a shop window.

_____ 4. Ron paused as the girl stopped at a shop window he had been following.

_____ 5. Marta dropped out of school after taking ten courses on Friday.

Handbook of Sentence Skills

_____ 6. On Friday, Marta dropped out of school after taking ten courses.

_____ 7. Under his shirt, the player wore a good luck charm that resembled a tiny elephant.

_____ 8. The player wore a good luck charm under his shirt that resembled a tiny elephant.

_____ 9. I ordered a new telephone from the mail-order catalog shaped like a cartoon character.

_____ 10. I ordered from the mail-order catalog a new telephone shaped like a cartoon character.

■ Review Test 2

Make the changes needed to correct the misplaced modifier in each sentence.

1. Henry Wadsworth Longfellow wrote that rainbows are flowers that have died and gone to heaven in a poem.

   _____

   _____

2. Because of the storm, I almost arrived two hours late for my first day on the job.

   _____

   _____

3. The apprentice watched the carpenter expertly fit the door with envious eyes.

   _____

   _____

4. The photographer pointed the camera at the shy deer equipped with a special night-vision scope.

   _____

   _____

5. The people on the bus stared at the ceiling or read newspapers with tired faces.

   _____

   _____

33 Dangling Modifiers

16.4

A modifier that opens a sentence must be followed immediately by the word it is meant to describe. Otherwise, the modifier is said to be dangling, and the sentence takes on an unintended meaning. For example, in the sentence

> While reading the newspaper, my dog sat with me on the front steps.

the unintended meaning is that the *dog* was reading the paper. What the writer meant, of course, was that *he* (or *she*), the writer, was reading the paper. The writer should have said,

> While reading the newspaper, *I* sat with my dog on the front steps.

The dangling modifier could also be corrected by placing the subject within the opening word group:

> While *I* was reading the newspaper, my dog sat with me on the front steps.

Here are other sentences with dangling modifiers. Read the explanations of why they are dangling, and look carefully at how they are corrected.

Dangling	Correct
Shaving in front of the steamy mirror, the razor nicked Ed's chin.	Shaving in front of the steamy mirror, *Ed* nicked his chin with the razor.
(*Who* was shaving in front of the mirror? The answer is not *razor* but *Ed*. The subject *Ed* must be added.)	*Or:* When *Ed* was shaving in front of the steamy mirror, he nicked his chin with the razor.
While turning over the bacon, hot grease splashed my arm.	While *I* was turning over the bacon, hot grease splashed my arm.
(*Who* is turning over the bacon? The answer is not *hot grease,* as it unintentionally seems to be, but *I*. The subject *I* must be added.)	*Or:* While turning over the bacon, *I* was splashed by hot grease.

Handbook of Sentence Skills

Dangling	**Correct**
Taking the exam, the room was so stuffy that Keisha almost fainted. (*Who* took the exam? The answer is not *the room* but *Keisha*. The subject *Keisha* must follow the modifier.)	Taking the exam, *Keisha* found the room so stuffy that she almost fainted. *Or:* When *Keisha* took the exam, the room was so stuffy that she almost fainted.
To impress the interviewer, punctuality is essential. (*Who* is to impress the interviewer? The answer is not *punctuality* but *you*. The subject *you* must be added.)	To impress the interviewer, *you* must be punctual. *Or:* For *you* to impress the interviewer, punctuality is essential.

The examples above show two ways of correcting a dangling modifier. Decide on a logical subject and do one of the following:

1   Place the subject *within* the opening word group:

When *Ed* was shaving in front of the steamy mirror, he nicked his chin.

Note   In some cases, an appropriate subordinating word such as *when* must be added and the verb may have to be changed slightly as well.

2   Place the subject right *after* the opening word group:

Shaving in front of the steamy mirror, *Ed* nicked his chin.

ACTIVITY

Look at the opening words in each sentence and ask, *Who?* The subject that answers the question should be nearby in the sentence. If it is not, provide the logical subject by using either method of correction described above.

EXAMPLE   While pitching his tent, a snake bit Tony on the ankle.

While Tony was pitching his tent, a snake bit him on the ankle.

Or: _While pitching his tent, Tony was bitten on the ankle by a snake._

Dangling Modifiers

1. Dancing on their hind legs, the audience cheered wildly as the elephants paraded by.

   _____

   _____

2. Last seen wearing dark glasses and a blond wig, the police spokesperson said the suspect was still being sought.

   _____

   _____

3. Pouring out the cereal, a coupon fell into my bowl of milk.

   _____

   _____

4. Escorted by dozens of police motorcycles, I knew the limousine carried someone important.

   _____

   _____

5. Tired and exasperated, the fight we had was inevitable.

   _____

   _____

6. Packed tightly in a tiny can, Fran had difficulty removing the anchovies.

   _____

   _____

7. Kicked carelessly under the bed, Raquel finally found her sneakers.

   _____

   _____

8. Working at the Xerox machine, the morning dragged on.

   _____

   _____

9. Sitting at a sidewalk café, all sorts of interesting people passed by.

   _____

   _____

10. Though somewhat warped, Uncle Zeke played his records from the forties.

    _____

    _____

Handbook of Sentence Skills

■ **Review Test 1**

Write DM for *dangling modifier* or C for *correct* in the space provided for each sentence.

_____ 1. While riding the bicycle, a vicious-looking German shepherd snapped at Tim's ankles.

_____ 2. While Tim was riding the bicycle, a vicious-looking German shepherd snapped at his ankles.

_____ 3. Afraid to look his father in the eye, Howard kept his head bowed.

_____ 4. Afraid to look his father in the eye, Howard's head remained bowed.

_____ 5. Boring and silly, I turned the TV show off.

_____ 6. I turned off the boring and silly TV show.

_____ 7. Munching leaves from a tall tree, the giraffe fascinated the children.

_____ 8. Munching leaves from a tall tree, the children were fascinated by the giraffe.

_____ 9. At the age of twelve, several colleges had already accepted the boy genius.

_____ 10. At the age of twelve, the boy genius had already been accepted by several colleges.

■ **Review Test 2**

Make the changes needed to correct the dangling modifier in each sentence.

1. Not having had much sleep, my concentration during class was weak.

   _____

   _____

2. Joined at the hip, a team of surgeons successfully separated the Siamese twins.

   _____

   _____

3. Wading in the shallow surf, a baby shark brushed past my leg.

   _____

   _____

4. While being restrained by federal marshals, the judge sentenced the kidnapper.

_____

_____

5. In a sentimental frame of mind, the music brought tears to Beth's eyes.

_____

_____

▪ Review Test 3

Complete the following sentences. In each case, a logical subject should follow the opening words.

EXAMPLE Looking through the door's peephole, *I couldn't see who rang the doorbell.*

1. Noticing the light turn yellow, _____

2. Being fragile, _____

3. While washing the car, _____

4. Although very expensive, _____

5. Driving past the cemetery, _____

Mechanics

34 Manuscript Form

When you hand in a paper for any course, it will probably be judged first by its format. It is important, then, to make the paper look attractive, neat, and easy to read. Here is a checklist you should use when preparing a paper for an instructor:

_____ • Is the paper full-size, 8½ by 11 inches?

_____ • Are there wide margins (1 to 1½ inches) all around the paper? In particular, have you been careful not to crowd the right-hand or bottom margin?

_____ • If the paper is handwritten, have you

Used a blue or black pen?

Been careful not to overlap letters or to make decorative loops on letters?

Made all your letters distinct, with special attention to *a, e, i, o,* and *u* —five letters that people sometimes write illegibly?

Kept all your capital letters clearly distinct from small letters?

_____ • Have you centered the title of your paper on the first line of page 1? Have you been careful *not* to put quotation marks around the title and *not* to underline it? Have you capitalized all the words in the title except short connecting words like *of, for, the, and, in,* and *to*?

_____ • Have you skipped a line between the title and the first line of your paper?

_____ • Have you indented the first line of each paragraph about five spaces (half an inch) from the left-hand margin?

_____ • Have you made commas, periods, and other punctuation marks firm and clear? If you are typing or keyboarding, have you left a double space after a period?

_____ • If you have broken any words at the end of a line, have you been careful to break only between syllables?

_____ • Have you put your name, the date, and other information at the end of the paper (or wherever your instructor has specified)?

Also ask yourself these important questions about the title and the first sentence of your paper:

____ • Is your title made up of several words that tell what the paper is about? (The title should be just several words, not a complete sentence.)

____ • Does the first sentence of your paper stand independent of the title? (The reader should *not* have to use the words in the title to make sense of the opening sentence.)

ACTIVITY

Use the checklist to locate the seven mistakes in format in the following lines from a student paper. Explain the mistakes in the spaces provided. One mistake is described for you as an example.

	"Being alone"
	This is something that I simply cannot tolerate, and I will predi-
	ctably go to great lengths to prevent it. For example, if I know that

1. Hyphenate only between syllables (predict-ably, not predi-ctably).

2. _____

3. _____

4. _____

5. _____

6. _____

7. _____

35 Capital Letters

Main Uses of Capital Letters

25.1

Capital letters are used with

1   First word in a sentence or direct quotation
2   Names of persons and the word *I*
3   Names of particular places
4   Names of days of the week, months, and holidays
5   Names of commercial products
6   Titles of books, magazines, newspapers, articles, stories, poems, films, television shows, songs, papers that you write, and the like
7   Names of companies, associations, unions, clubs, religious and political groups, and other organizations

Each use is illustrated in this chapter.

First Word in a Sentence or Direct Quotation

The corner grocery was robbed last night.

The alien said, "Take me to your leader."

"If you need help," said Teri, "call me. I'll be over in no time."

Note   In the third example above, *If* and *I'll* are capitalized because they start new sentences. But *call* is not capitalized, because it is part of the first sentence.

Names of Persons and the Word *I*

Last night, I saw a hilarious movie starring Stan Laurel and Oliver Hardy.

Names of Particular Places and Institutions

Although Bill dropped out of Port Charles High School, he eventually earned his degree and got a job with Atlas Realty Company.

But   Use small letters if the specific name is not given.

Although Bill dropped out of high school, he eventually earned his degree and got a job with a real estate company.

Names of Days of the Week, Months, and Holidays

On the last Friday afternoon in May, the day before Memorial Day, my boss is having a barbecue for all the employees.

But   Use small letters for the seasons—summer, fall, winter, spring.

Most people feel more energetic in the spring and fall.

Names of Commercial Products

Keith installed a new Sony stereo and a Motorola cell phone into his old Ford Ranger pickup.

But   Use small letters for the *type* of product (stereo, cell phone, pickup, and so on).

Titles of Books, Magazines, Newspapers, Articles, Stories, Poems, Films, Television Shows, Songs, Papers That You Write, and the Like

We read the book *Hiroshima*, by John Hersey, for our history class.

In the doctor's waiting room, I watched *All My Children*, read an article in *Reader's Digest*, and leafed through the *Miami Herald*.

Names of Companies, Associations, Unions, Clubs, Religious and Political Groups, and Other Organizations

Joe Naples is a Roman Catholic, but his wife is a Methodist.

The Hilldale Square Dancers' Club has won many competitions.

Brian, a member of Bricklayers Local 431 and the Knights of Columbus, works for Ace Construction.

Handbook of Sentence Skills

ACTIVITY

Underline the words that need capitals in the following sentences. Then write the capitalized form of each word in the space provided. The number of spaces tells you how many corrections to make in each case.

EXAMPLE In our biology class, each student must do a report on an article in the magazine *scientific american*. _Scientific_ _American_

1. Leon's collection of beatles souvenirs includes a pair of tickets from their last concert in candlestick park in San Francisco.

   _____ _____ _____

2. Yumi read in *natural health* magazine that abraham lincoln suffered from severe depression.

   _____ _____ _____ _____

3. When i have a cold, I use vick's ointment and chew listerine lozenges.

   _____ _____ _____

4. Since no man volunteered for the job, the boy scouts in springfield, illinois, have a woman troop leader.

   _____ _____ _____ _____ _____

5. A nature trail for the blind in cape cod, massachusetts, has signs written in Braille that encourage visitors to smell and touch the plants.

   _____ _____ _____

6. Some of the most popular items at a restaurant called big river are chilean sea bass and atlantic clam chowder.

   _____ _____ _____ _____

7. My father is a confirmed Dallas cowboys fan, though he lives in boston.

   _____ _____

8. Martha bought a diet pepsi to wash down her hostess twinkie.

   _____ _____ _____ _____

9. Vince listened to a U2 album called *The Joshua Tree* while Donna read an article in *glamour* titled "What Do men Really want?"

   _____ _____ _____

10. After having her baby, joan received a card from one of her friends that read, "congratulations, we all knew you had it in you."

    _____ _____

Other Uses of Capital Letters

Capital letters are also used with

1   Names that show family relationships
2   Titles of persons when used with their names
3   Specific school courses
4   Languages
5   Geographic locations
6   Historical periods and events
7   Races, nations, and nationalities
8   Opening and closing of a letter

Each use is illustrated below.

Names That Show Family Relationships

All his life, Father has been addicted to gadgets.

I browsed through Grandmother's collection of old photographs.

Aunt Florence and Uncle Bill bought a mobile home.

But   Do not capitalize words like *mother, father, grandmother, grandfather, uncle, aunt,* and so on when they are preceded by a possessive word (such as *my, your, his, her, our, their*).

All his life, my father has been addicted to gadgets.

I browsed through my grandmother's collection of old photographs.

My aunt and uncle bought a mobile home.

Titles of Persons When Used with Their Names

I contributed to Senator McGrath's campaign fund.

Is Dr. Gomez on vacation?

Professor Adams announced that there would be no tests in the course.

But   Use lowercase letters when titles appear by themselves, without specific names.

I contributed to my senator's campaign fund.

Is the doctor on vacation?

The professor announced that there would be no tests in the course.

Specific School Courses

The college offers evening sections of Introductory Psychology I, Abnormal Psychology, Psychology and Statistics, and Educational Psychology.

But   Use lowercase letters for general subject areas.

The college offers evening sections of many psychology courses.

Languages

My grandfather's Polish accent makes his English difficult to understand.

Geographic Locations

He grew up in the Midwest but moved to the South to look for a better job.

But   Use lowercase letters in directions.

Head west for five blocks and then turn south on State Street.

Historical Periods and Events

During the Middle Ages, the Black Death killed over one-quarter of Europe's population.

Races, Nations, and Nationalities

The questionnaire asked if the head of our household was Caucasian, African American, Asian, Latino, or Native American.

Tanya has lived on army bases in Germany, Italy, and Spain.

Denise's beautiful features reflect her Chinese and Mexican parentage.

Opening and Closing of a Letter

Dear Sir:	Sincerely yours,
Dear Ms. Henderson:	Truly yours,

Note   Capitalize only the first word in a closing.

Capital Letters

ACTIVITY

Underline the words that need capitals in the following sentences. Then write the capitalized forms of the words in the spaces provided. The number of spaces tells you how many corrections to make in each case.

1. During world war II, many americans were afraid that the japanese would invade California.

   _____ _____ _____ _____

2. On their job site in korea, the french, swiss, and chinese coworkers used English to communicate.

   _____ _____ _____ _____

3. When uncle harvey got the bill from his doctor, he called the American Medical Association to complain.

   _____ _____

4. Dr. Freeling of the business department is offering a new course called introduction to web design.

   _____ _____ _____

5. A new restaurant featuring vietnamese cuisine has just opened on the south side of the city.

   _____

Unnecessary Use of Capitals

ACTIVITY

Many errors in capitalization are caused by using capitals where they are not needed. Underline the incorrectly capitalized words in the following sentences, and write the correct forms in the spaces provided. The number of spaces tells you how many corrections to make in each sentence.

1. George Washington's Forces starved at Valley Forge because Pennsylvania Farmers preferred to sell food to the British for cash.

   _____ _____

2. The virus damaged the files on my Brother's Dell Computer.

   _____ _____

Handbook of Sentence Skills

3. The country cheered in the summer of 1998 when Mark McGwire of the St. Louis Cardinals Baseball Team broke the single-season Home Run record set by Roger Maris.

_____   _____   _____   _____

4. In his Book titled *Offbeat Museums,* Saul Rubin tells about various Unusual Museums, such as, Believe it or not, the Kansas Barbed Wire Museum.

_____   _____   _____   _____

5. Einstein's theory of relativity, which he developed when he was only twenty-six, led to the invention of the Electron Microscope, Television, and the Atomic bomb.

_____   _____   _____   _____

■ Review Test 1

Add capitals where needed in the following sentences.

EXAMPLE In an injured tone, Mary demanded, "why wasn't uncle Lou invited to the party?"
(with handwritten corrections: W above "why", U above "uncle")

1. To keep warm, a homeless old man sits on a steam vent near hampton park on tenth street.

2. Silent movie stars of the twenties, like charlie chaplin and gloria swanson, earned more than a million tax-free dollars a year.

3. Insects living in mammoth cave in kentucky include blind crickets, spiders, and flies.

4. When former president Bill Clinton was a boy in arkansas, he was photographed shaking hands with president John F. Kennedy.

5. In an old movie, an attractive young lady invites groucho marx to join her.

6. "why?" asks groucho. "are you coming apart?"

7. I was halfway to the wash & dry Laundromat on elm street when i realized that my box of tide was still home on the kitchen counter.

8. Although I know that mother loves holidays, even I was surprised when she announced a party in february to celebrate groundhog day.

9. *Rolling stone* magazine features an article about plans to remake the Alfred Hitchcock classic *the birds* and a review of a new biography about elvis presley.

10. Celebrities have earned big money by endorsing products, including nike shoes, trident gum, and jell-O pudding.

■ Review Test 2

On separate paper, write

1. Seven sentences demonstrating the seven main uses of capital letters.
2. Eight sentences demonstrating the eight other uses of capital letters.

36 Numbers and Abbreviations

Numbers

25.2

Here are three helpful rules for using numbers.

Rule 1   Spell out numbers that take no more than two words. Otherwise, use the numbers themselves.

> In Jody's kitchen is her collection of seventy-two cookbooks.
>
> Jody has a file of 350 recipes.
>
> It will take about two weeks to fix the computer database.
>
> Since a number of people use the database, the company will lose over 150 workdays.
>
> Only twelve students have signed up for the field trip.
>
> Nearly 250 students came to the lecture.

Rule 2   Be consistent when you use a series of numbers. If some numbers in a sentence or paragraph require more than two words, then use numbers for the others, too.

> After the storm, maintenance workers unclogged 46 drains, removed 123 broken tree limbs, and rescued 3 kittens who were stuck in a drainpipe.

Rule 3   Use numbers to show dates, times, addresses, percentages, and chapters of a book.

> The burglary was committed on October 30, 2003, but not discovered until January 2, 2004.
>
> Before I went to bed, I set my alarm for 6:45 A.M. (*But:* Spell out numbers before *o'clock*. For example: I didn't get out of bed until seven o'clock.)
>
> The library is located at 45 West 52nd Street.

When you take the skin off a piece of chicken, you remove about 40 percent of the fat.

The name of the murderer is revealed in Chapter 8 on page 236.

ACTIVITY

Cross out the mistakes in numbers and write the corrections in the spaces provided.

1. The Puerto Rican Pride Parade will begin at three-thirty in front of the newspaper office at one-oh-six South Forty-Second Street.

   _____ _____ _____

2. It took 4 hours to proofread all 75 pages of the manuscript.

   _____ _____

3. We expect to have fifty percent of the work completed by March tenth.

   _____ _____

Abbreviations

Using abbreviations can save you time when you take notes. In formal writing, however, you should avoid most abbreviations. Listed below are some of the few abbreviations that are considered acceptable in compositions. Note that a period is used after most abbreviations.

1   Mr., Mrs., Ms., Jr., Sr., Dr. when used with names:

   Mrs. Johnson   Dr. Garcia   Howard Kelley, Jr.

2   Time references:

   A.M. or a.m.   P.M. or p.m.   B.C., A.D.

3   Initials in a person's name:

   J. Edgar Hoover   John F. Kennedy   Michael J. Fox

4   Organizations, technical words, and company names known primarily by their initials:

   IBM   UNICEF   ABC   IRS   NBA   AIDS

Handbook of Sentence Skills

ACTIVITY

Cross out the words that should not be abbreviated, and correct them in the spaces provided.

1. Between mid-Nov. and the beginning of Jan., I typically gain about five lbs.

   _____   _____   _____

2. I had such a bad headache this aftern. that I called my doc. for an appt.

   _____   _____   _____

3. I stopped at the p.o. at about twenty min. past ten and bought five dol. worth of stamps.

   _____   _____   _____   _____

Review Test

Cross out the mistakes in numbers and abbreviations, and correct them in the spaces provided.

1. Sanjay was shocked when he transferred from a small h.s. to one with over 5,000 students.

   _____   _____   _____   _____

2. Grandpa lived to be ninety-nine despite smoking 3 packs of cigs. every day.

   _____   _____

3. Although the 2 girls are twins, they have different birthdays: one was born just before midnight on Feb. twenty-fifth and the other a few minutes later, after midnight.

   _____   _____   _____

4. In their first week of Span. class, students learned to count from 1 to twenty-one and studied Chapter One in their textbook.

   _____   _____   _____

5. When I cleaned out the junk drawer in the kitch., I found twelve rubber bands, thirty-seven paper clips, and 3 used-up batteries.

   _____   _____

Punctuation

37 Apostrophe

24.6

The two main uses of the apostrophe are

1   To show the omission of one or more letters in a contraction

2   To show ownership or possession

Each use is explained in this chapter.

Apostrophe in Contractions

A *contraction* is formed when two words are combined to make one word. An apostrophe is used to show where letters are omitted in forming the contraction. Here are two contractions:

> have + not = haven't (the *o* in *not* has been omitted)
> I + will = I'll (the *wi* in *will* has been omitted)

Following are some other common contractions:

I + am = I'm	it + is = it's
I + have = I've	it + has = it's
I + had = I'd	is + not = isn't
who + is = who's	could + not = couldn't
do + not = don't	I + would = I'd
did + not = didn't	they + are = they're

Note   Will + not has an unusual contraction: won't.

Handbook of Sentence Skills

ACTIVITY

Write the contractions for the words in parentheses. One is done for you.

1. (Are not) _____Aren't_____ the reserve books in the library kept at the circulation desk?

2. If (they are) _____ coming over, (I had) _____ better cook more hot dogs.

3. (I am) _____ the kind of student (who is) _____ extremely nervous before tests.

4. (We are) _____ hoping to find out (who is) _____ responsible for this error; (it is) _____ important to us to keep our customers happy.

5. I (can not) _____ remember if (there is) _____ gas in the car or not.

Note   Even though contractions are common in everyday speech and in written dialogue, it is often best to avoid them in formal writing.

Apostrophe to Show Ownership or Possession

To show ownership or possession, we can use such words as *belongs to, possessed by, owned by,* or (most commonly) *of.*

the umbrella *that belongs to* Mark

the toys *possessed by* children

the tape recorder *owned by* the school

the gentleness *of* my father

But the apostrophe plus *s* (if the word does not end in *s*) is often the quickest and easiest way to show possession. Thus we can say

Mark's umbrella

children's toys

the school's tape recorder

my father's gentleness

Points to Remember

1 The *'s* goes with the owner or possessor (in the examples given, *Mark, children, the school, my father*). What follows is the person or thing possessed (in the examples given, *the umbrella, the toys, the tape recorder, gentleness*).

2 There should always be a break between the word and *'s*.

Mark's   not   Marks

Yes   No

3 An apostrophe plus *s* is used to show possession with a singular word even if the word already ends in *s*: for example, Doris's purse (the purse belonging to Doris).

ACTIVITY 1

Rewrite the *italicized* part of each of the sentences below, using *'s* to show possession. Remember that the *'s* goes with the owner or possessor.

EXAMPLE *The wing of the bluejay* was broken.

The bluejay's wing was broken.

1. *The annoying voice of the comedian* irritated me, so I changed the TV channel.

   _____

2. *The performance of the quarterback* is inconsistent.

   _____

3. *The thin hand belonging to the old woman* felt as dry as parchment.

   _____

4. *In the window of the jewelry store* is a sign reading "Ears Pierced While You Wait."

   _____

5. A fly flew into *the mouth of the TV weatherperson.*

   _____

6. *The new denim shirt belonging to Lamont* was as scratchy as sandpaper.

   _____

7. *The hair belonging to Rachel* is usually not green—she colored it for Halloween.

_____

8. *The bowl of cereal belonging to Dennis* refused to snap, crackle, or pop.

_____

9. *The Honda owned by Donna* was crammed with boxes and furniture.

_____

10. *The previous tenant of the apartment* had painted all the walls bright green.

_____

ACTIVITY 2

Add *'s* to each of the following words to make it the possessor or owner of something. Then write sentences using the words. The first one is done for you.

1. rock star ____*rock star's*____

   The rock star's limousine pulled up to the curb.

2. Felipe _____

   _____

3. pilot _____

   _____

4. neighbor _____

   _____

5. school _____

   _____

6. gunslinger _____

   _____

Apostrophe versus Possessive Pronouns

Do not use an apostrophe with possessive pronouns. They already show ownership. Possessive pronouns include *his, hers, its, yours, ours,* and *theirs.*

Incorrect	Correct
The sun warped his' albums.	The sun warped his albums.
The restored Model T is theirs'.	The restored Model T is theirs.
The decision is yours'.	The decision is yours.
The plaid suitcase is ours'.	The plaid suitcase is ours.
The lion charged its' prey.	The lion charged its prey.

Apostrophe versus Simple Plurals

When you want to make a word plural, just add an *s* at the end of the word. Do not add an apostrophe. For example, the plural of the word *movie* is *movies,* not *movie's* or *movies'*.

Look at this sentence:

Tim coveted his roommate's collection of cassette tapes and compact discs.

The words *tapes* and *discs* are simple plurals, meaning more than one tape, more than one disc. The plural is shown by adding *s* only. On the other hand, the *'s* after *roommate* shows possession—that the roommate owns the tapes and discs.

ACTIVITY

Insert an apostrophe where needed to show possession in the following sentences. Write *plural* above words where the *s* ending simply means more than one thing.

EXAMPLE   Arlene's tinted contact lenses protect her eyes from glare.

1. Harry grasped his wifes arm as she stood on in-line skates for the first time.

2. Vonettes decision to study computer science is based on predictions of good opportunities for women in that field.

3. The fires extreme heat had melted the telephones in the office and welded the metal chairs into a twisted heap.

4. At the doctors request, Lyndon pulled up his shirt and revealed the zipperlike scars from his operation.

5. Of all the peoples names in all the worlds countries, the most common is Muhammad.

6. At the end of the day, Hals shirt and pants smelled like gasoline, and his fingernails were rimmed with grease.

7. The childrens shouts of delight grew louder as the clown added eggs, lightbulbs, and a bowling ball to the items he was juggling.

8. Tinas camping handbook suggests that we bring water purification tablets and nylon ropes.

9. Carmens leaky pen had stained her fingers a deep blue.

10. The rattlesnakes head has a sensitive pit below the eyes, capable of detecting the body heat of warm-blooded prey.

Apostrophe with Plurals Ending in -s

Plurals that end in -s show possession simply by adding the apostrophe, rather than an apostrophe plus s.

the Thompsons' porch
the players' victory
her parents' motor home
the Rolling Stones' last CD
the soldiers' hats

ACTIVITY

Add an apostrophe where needed.

1. Several campers tents collapsed during the storm.

2. The Murrays phone bills are often over $100 a month.

3. Many buildings steep steps make it difficult for wheelchair users to gain access.

4. The twins habit of dressing alike was started by their mother when they were children.

5. At the crowded intersection, several young men rushed out to wash the cars windshields.

102

■ Review Test

In each sentence, underline the two words that need apostrophes. Then write the words correctly in the spaces provided.

_____
_____

1. The sagging sofas stuffing was coming out in several places, and one of the chairs legs was broken.

_____
_____

2. A shaky rope ladder led from the barns wooden floor to the haylofts dusty shadows.

_____
_____

3. The paperback books glaring purple and orange cover was designed to attract a hurrying customers eye.

_____
_____

4. Sofias essay was due in a matter of hours, but she suffered writers block that emptied her brain.

_____
_____

5. While he waited in his bosss office, Charlies nervous fingers shredded a Styrofoam coffee cup into a pile of jagged white flakes.

_____
_____

6. Gregory couldnt remember whether he had left his wallet in his cars glove compartment or at home.

_____
_____

7. Members of the parents association constructed a maze made of old tires for the childrens playground.

_____
_____

8. The cats great green eyes grew even wider as the curious dogs sniffing nose came too close to her.

_____
_____

9. The suns rays beat down until the streets blacktopped surface softened with the heat.

_____
_____

10. The rivers swirling floodwaters lapped against the Hendersons porch.

38 Quotation Marks

24.3

The two main uses of quotation marks are

1   To set off the exact words of a speaker or writer
2   To set off the titles of short works

Each use is explained here.

Quotation Marks to Set Off the Words of a Speaker or Writer

Use quotation marks to show the exact words of a speaker or writer.

"I feel as though I've been here before," Angie murmured to her husband.

(Quotation marks set off the exact words that Angie spoke to her husband.)

Ben Franklin once wrote, "To lengthen thy life, lessen thy meals."

(Quotation marks set off the exact words that Ben Franklin wrote.)

"Did you know," said the nutrition expert, "that it's healthier to be ten pounds overweight?"

(Two pairs of quotation marks are used to enclose the nutrition expert's exact words.)

The biology professor said, "Ants are a lot like human beings. They farm their own food and raise smaller insects as livestock. And, like humans, ants send armies to war."

(Note that the end quotation marks do not come until the end of the biology professor's speech. Place quotation marks before the first quoted word and after the last quoted word. As long as no interruption occurs in the speech, do not use quotation marks for each new sentence.)

Quotation Marks

Punctuation Hint   In the four examples above, notice that a comma sets the quoted part off from the rest of the sentence. Also, observe that commas and periods at the end of a quotation always go *inside* quotation marks.

Complete the following statements, which explain how capital letters, commas, and periods are used in quotations. Refer to the four examples as guides.

1. Every quotation begins with a _____ letter.

2. When a quotation is split (as in the sentence about the nutrition expert), the

   second part does not begin with a capital letter unless it is a _____ sentence.

3. _____ are used to separate the quoted part of a sentence from the rest of the sentence.

4. Commas and periods that come at the end of a quotation go _____ the quotation marks.

The answers are *capital, new, Commas,* and *inside.*

ACTIVITY 1

Place quotation marks around the exact words of a speaker or writer in the sentences that follow.

1. Several people have been credited with saying, The more I see of people, the more I like dogs.

2. Beatrice asked, Do you give a discount to senior citizens?

3. This hamburger is raw! cried Leon.

4. The bumper sticker on the rear of the battered old car read, Don't laugh—it's paid for.

5. I know why Robin Hood robbed only the rich, said the comedian. The poor don't have any money.

6. These CDs, proclaimed the television announcer, are not sold in any store.

7. When chefs go to great lengths, the woman at the diet center said, I go to great widths.

8. If I go with you to the dinner party, my friend said, you must promise not to discuss politics.

9. On a tombstone in a Maryland cemetery are the words Here lies an atheist, all dressed up and no place to go.

10. The columnist advised, Be nice to people on your way up because you'll meet them on your way down.

Handbook of Sentence Skills

ACTIVITY 2

1. Write a sentence in which you quote a favorite expression of someone you know. In the same sentence, identify the person's relationship to you.

   EXAMPLE *My grandfather loves to say, "It can't be as bad as all that."*

   _____

   _____

   _____

   _____

2. Write a quotation that contains the words *Pablo asked Teresa*. Write a second quotation that includes the words *Teresa replied*.

   _____

   _____

   _____

   _____

   _____

   _____

   _____

   _____

   _____

3. Quote an interesting sentence or two from a book or magazine. In the same sentence, identify the title and author of the work.

   EXAMPLE *In The Dilbert Desk Calendar by Scott Adams, the cartoon character Dilbert says, "I can please only one person per day. Today isn't your day, and tomorrow isn't looking good either."*

   _____

   _____

   _____

   _____

   _____

   _____

   _____

   _____

   _____

   _____

Indirect Quotations

An indirect quotation is a rewording of someone else's comments rather than a word-for-word direct quotation. The word *that* often signals an indirect quotation.

Direct Quotation	Indirect Quotation
The nurse said, "Some babies cannot tolerate cows' milk."	The nurse said that some babies cannot tolerate cows' milk.
(The nurse's exact spoken words are given, so quotation marks are used.)	(We learn the nurse's words indirectly, so no quotation marks are used.)
Vicky's note to Dan read, "I'll be home by 7:30."	Vicky left a note for Dan saying that she would be home by 7:30.
(The exact words that Vicky wrote in the note are given, so quotation marks are used.)	(We learn Vicky's words indirectly, so no quotation marks are used.)

ACTIVITY

Rewrite the following sentences, changing words as necessary to convert the sentences into direct quotations. The first one has been done for you as an example.

1. Teddy asked Margie if she wanted to see his spider collection.

   Teddy asked Margie, "Do you want to see my spider collection?"

2. Sonya said that her uncle looks just like a large basset hound.

   _____

3. Angelo said that he wanted a box of the extra-crispy chicken.

   _____

4. My boss told me that I could make mistakes as long as I didn't repeat them.

   _____

5. The instructor announced that Thursday's test had been canceled.

   _____

Handbook of Sentence Skills

Quotation Marks to Set Off Titles of Short Works

24.3c

Titles of short works are usually set off by quotation marks, while titles of long works are underlined. Use quotation marks to set off titles of such short works as articles in books, newspapers, or magazines; chapters in a book; short stories; poems; and songs. But you should underline titles of books, newspapers, magazines, plays, movies, CDs, and television shows. Following are some examples.

Quotation Marks	Underlines
the essay "On Self-Respect"	in the book <u>Slouching Towards Bethlehem</u>
the article "The Problem of Acid Rain"	in the newspaper <u>The New York Times</u>
the article "Living with Inflation"	in the magazine <u>Newsweek</u>
the chapter "Chinese Religion"	in the book <u>Paths of Faith</u>
the story "Hands"	in the book <u>Winesburg, Ohio</u>
the poem "When I Have Fears"	in the book <u>Complete Poems of John Keats</u>
the song "Ziggy Stardust"	in the CD <u>Changes</u>
	the television show <u>60 Minutes</u>
	the movie <u>High Noon</u>

Note   In printed works, including papers that are prepared on a computer, italic type—slanted type that looks *like this*—is used instead of underlining.

ACTIVITY

Use quotation marks or underlines as needed.

1. In her short story A Sea Worry, Maxine Hong Kingston describes a group of teenage surfers and a mother who tries to understand them.

2. I bought the National Enquirer to read an article titled Painful Beauty Secrets of the Stars.

3. We read the chapter Pulling Up Roots in Gail Sheehy's book Passages.

4. Jamila used an article titled Winter Blues from Time magazine in her research paper about seasonal depression.

5. The movie Casablanca, which starred Humphrey Bogart, was originally cast with Ronald Reagan in the leading role.

6. One of my grandfather's favorite old TV shows was Thriller, a horror series hosted by Boris Karloff, the man who starred in the 1931 movie Frankenstein.

7. When the Beatles' movie A Hard Day's Night was first shown, fans screamed so much that no one could hear the songs or the dialogue.

8. On my father's wall is a framed front page of The New York Times of February 25, 1940—the day he was born.

9. The sociology test will cover the first two chapters: Culture and Diversity and Social Stratification.

10. An article in Consumer Reports called Which Cereal for Breakfast? claims that children can learn to like low-sugar cereals like Cheerios and Wheaties.

Other Uses of Quotation Marks

Quotation marks are also used as follows:

1 To set off special words or phrases from the rest of a sentence:

In grade school, we were taught a little jingle about the spelling rule "*i* before *e*."

What is the difference between "it's" and "its"?

(In this book, *italics* are often used instead of quotation marks to set off words.)

2 To mark off a quotation within a quotation:

24.3a

The physics professor said, "For class on Friday, do the problems at the end of the chapter titled 'Work and Energy.'"

Brendan remarked, "Did you know that Humphrey Bogart never actually said, 'Play it again, Sam' in the movie *Casablanca*?"

Note   A quotation within a quotation is indicated by *single* quotation marks, as shown above.

Handbook of Sentence Skills

Review Test 1

Insert quotation marks where needed in the sentences that follow.

1. The psychology class read a short story called Silent Snow, Secret Snow, about a young boy who creates his own fantasy world.

2. While filming the movie *Vertigo,* the actress Kim Novak was agonizing over how to play a particular scene until the director, Alfred Hitchcock, reminded her, Kim, it's only a movie!

3. I'm against grade school students' using pocket calculators, said Fred. I spent three years learning long division, and so should they.

4. The composer George Gershwin wrote many hundreds of hit songs, including classics like Summertime and Somebody Loves Me.

5. When I gagged while taking a foul-tasting medicine, my wife said, Put an ice cube on your tongue first, and then you won't taste it.

6. I looked twice at the newspaper headline that read, Man in River Had Drinking Problem.

7. To learn more about the stock market for his business class, Jared began reading the column by Pablo Galarza in *Money* magazine called MarketRap.

8. When a guest at the wedding was asked what he was giving the couple, he replied, About six months.

9. Theodore Roosevelt, a pioneer in conservation, once said, When I hear of the destruction of a species, I feel as if all the works of some great writer had perished.

10. If you're ever in trouble, said the police officer, you'll have a better chance of attracting aid if you shout Fire instead of Help.

Review Test 2

Go through the comics section of a newspaper to find a comic strip that amuses you. Be sure to choose a strip where two or more characters are speaking to each other. Write a full description that will enable people who have not read the comic strip to visualize it clearly and appreciate its humor. Describe the setting and action in each panel, and enclose the words of the speakers in quotation marks.

39 Comma

Six Main Uses of the Comma

23.2

Commas are used mainly as follows:

1. To separate items in a series
2. To set off introductory material
3. On both sides of words that interrupt the flow of thought in a sentence
4. Between two complete thoughts connected by *and, but, for, or, nor, so, yet*
5. To set off a direct quotation from the rest of a sentence
6. For certain everyday material

You may find it helpful to remember that the comma often marks a slight pause or break in a sentence. Read aloud the sentence examples given for each rule, and listen for the minor pauses or breaks that are signaled by commas.

1 Comma between Items in a Series

Use commas to separate items in a series.

> The street vendor sold watches, necklaces, and earrings.
> The pitcher adjusted his cap, pawed the ground, and peered over his shoulder.
> The exercise instructor told us to inhale, exhale, and relax.
> Joe peered into the hot, still-smoking engine.

Notes

a The final comma in a series is optional, but it is often used.

b A comma is used between two descriptive words in a series only if *and* inserted between the words sounds natural. You could say:

> Joe peered into the hot *and* still-smoking engine.

But notice in the following sentence that the descriptive words do not sound natural when *and* is inserted between them. In such cases, no comma is used.

Tony wore a pale green tuxedo. (A pale *and* green tuxedo does not sound right, so no comma is used.)

ACTIVITY

Place commas between items in a series.

1. The old kitchen cabinets were littered with dead insects crumbs and dust balls.
2. Rudy stretched out on the swaying hammock popped open a frosty can of soda and balanced it carefully on his stomach.
3. The children splashed through the warm deep swirling rainwater that flooded the street.
4. The police officer's warm brown eyes relaxed manner and pleasant smile made her easy to talk to.
5. The musty shadowy cellar with the crumbling cement floor was our favorite playground.

2 Comma after Introductory Material

Use a comma to set off introductory material.

Just in time, Sherry applied the brakes and avoided a car accident.

Muttering under his breath, Hassan reviewed the terms he had memorized.

In a wolf pack, the dominant male holds his tail higher than the other pack members.

Although he had been first in the checkout line, Deion let an elderly woman go ahead of him.

After the fire, we slogged through the ashes of the burned-out house.

Note   If the introductory material is brief, the comma is sometimes omitted. In the activities here, you should include the comma.

ACTIVITY

Place commas after introductory material.

1. As Patty struggled with the stuck window gusts of cold rain blew in her face.

2. His heart pounding wildly Jesse opened the letter that would tell him whether or not he had been accepted at college.

3. Along the once-pretty river people had dumped old tires and loads of household trash.

4. When the band hadn't taken the stage forty-five minutes after the concert was supposed to begin the audience members started shouting and stamping their feet.

5. Setting down a smudged glass of murky water the waitress tossed Darren a greasy menu and asked if he'd care to order.

3 Comma around Words Interrupting the Flow of Thought

Use a comma on both sides of words or phrases that interrupt the flow of thought in a sentence.

The vinyl car seat, sticky from the heat, clung to my skin.

Marty's computer, which his wife got him as a birthday gift, occupies all of his spare time.

The hallway, dingy and dark, was illuminated by a bare bulb hanging from a wire.

Usually, by reading a sentence aloud, you can "hear" words that interrupt the flow of thought. In cases where you are not sure if certain words are interrupters, remove them from the sentence. If it still makes sense without the words, you know that the words are interrupters and that the information they give is nonessential. *Such nonessential or extra information is set off with commas.*

In the sentence

Sue Dodd, who goes to aerobics class with me, was in a serious car accident.

the words *who goes to aerobics class with me* are extra information not needed to identify the subject of the sentence, *Sue Dodd*. Commas go around such nonessential information. On the other hand, in the sentence

The woman who goes to aerobics class with me was in a serious accident.

the words *who goes to aerobics class with me* supply essential information—information needed for us to identify the woman being spoken of. If the words were removed from the sentence, we would no longer know exactly who was in the accident: "The woman was in a serious accident." Here is another example:

> *Watership Down,* a novel by Richard Adams, is the most thrilling adventure story I've ever read.

Here the words *a novel by Richard Adams* could be left out, and we would still know the basic meaning of the sentence. Commas are placed around such nonessential material. But in the sentence

> Richard Adams's novel *Watership Down* is the most thrilling adventure story I've ever read.

the title of the novel is essential. Without it the sentence would read, "Richard Adams's novel is the most thrilling adventure story I've ever read." We would not know which of Richard Adams's novels was so thrilling. Commas are not used around the title, because it provides essential information.

Most of the time you will be able to "hear" words that interrupt the flow of thought in a sentence and will not have to think about whether the words are essential or nonessential.

ACTIVITY

Use commas to set off interrupting words.

1. A slight breeze hot and damp ruffled the bedroom curtains.
2. The defrosting chickens loosely wrapped in plastic left a pool on the counter.
3. Lenny's wallet which he kept in his front pants pocket was linked to his belt with a metal chain.
4. Mr. Delgado who is an avid Yankees fan remembers the grand days of Mickey Mantle and Yogi Berra.
5. The fleet of tall ships a majestic sight made its way into the harbor.

4 Comma between Complete Thoughts

Use a comma between two complete thoughts connected by *and, but, for, or, nor, so, yet.*

> Sam closed all the windows, but the predicted thunderstorm never arrived.
> I like wearing comfortable clothing, so I buy oversize shirts and sweaters.
> Peggy doesn't envy the skinny models in magazines, for she is happy with her own well-rounded body.

Notes

a The comma is optional when the complete thoughts are short.

> The Ferris wheel started and Wilson closed his eyes.
>
> Many people left but the band played on.
>
> I made a wrong turn so I doubled back.

b Be careful not to use a comma to separate two verbs that belong to one subject. The comma is used only in sentences made up of two complete thoughts (two subjects and two verbs). In the sentence

> The doctor stared over his bifocals and lectured me about smoking.

there is only one subject (*doctor*) and a double verb (*stared* and *lectured*). No comma is needed. Likewise, the sentence

> Dean switched the lamp on and off and then tapped it with his fingers.

has only one subject (*Dean*) and a double verb (*switched* and *tapped*); therefore, no comma is needed.

ACTIVITY

Place a comma before a joining word that connects two complete thoughts (two subjects and two verbs). Remember, do *not* place a comma within a sentence that has only one subject and a double verb. (Some items may be correct as given.)

1. The television sitcom was interrupted for a special news bulletin and I poked my head out of the kitchen to listen to the announcement.
2. The puppy was beaten by its former owner and cringes at the sound of a loud voice.
3. The eccentric woman brought all her own clips and rollers to the beauty parlor for she was afraid to use the ones there.
4. The tuna sandwich in my lunch is crushed and the cream-filled cupcake is plastered to the bottom of the bag.
5. The landlord promised repeatedly to come and fix the leaking shower but three months later he hasn't done a thing.
6. Ruth was tired of summer reruns so she visited the town library to pick up some interesting books.

7. You can spend hours driving all over town to look for a particular type of camera or you can telephone a few stores to find it quickly.

8. Many people strolled among the exhibits at the comic book collectors' convention and stopped to look at a rare first edition of *Superman.*

9. Our neighborhood crime patrol escorts elderly people to the local bank and installs free dead-bolt locks on their apartment doors.

10. Brendan tapped the small geraniums out of their pots and carefully planted them on his grandfather's grave.

5 Comma with Direct Quotations

Use a comma to set off a direct quotation from the rest of a sentence.

The carnival barker cried, "Step right up and win a prize!"

"Now is the time to yield to temptation," my horoscope read.

"I'm sorry," said the restaurant hostess. "You'll have to wait."

"For my first writing assignment," said Scott, "I have to turn in a five-hundred-word description of a stone."

Note   Commas and periods at the end of a quotation go inside quotation marks. See also page 509.

ACTIVITY

Use commas to set off direct quotations from the rest of the sentence.

1. The coach announced "In order to measure your lung capacity, you're going to attempt to blow up a plastic bag with one breath."

2. "A grapefruit" said the comedian "is a lemon that had a chance and took advantage of it."

3. My father asked "Did you know that the family moving next door has thirteen children?"

4. "Speak louder" a man in the back row said to the guest speaker. "I paid five dollars to hear you talk, not whisper."

5. The zookeeper explained to the visitors "We can't tell the sex of a giant tortoise for almost ten years after its birth."

6 Comma with Everyday Material

Use a comma with certain everyday material.

Persons Spoken To

If you're the last to leave, Paul, please switch off the lights.

Fred, I think we're on the wrong road.

Did you see the playoff game, Lisa?

Dates

June 30, 2008, is the day I make the last payment on my car.

Addresses

I buy discount children's clothing from Isaacs Baby Wear Factory, Box 900, Chicago, Illinois 60614.

Note   No comma is used before a zip code.

Openings and Closings of Letters

Dear Santa,   Sincerely yours,

Dear Roberto,   Truly yours,

Note   In formal letters, a colon is used after the opening:
Dear Sir: *or* Dear Madam: *or* Dear Allan: *or* Dear Ms. Mohr:

Numbers

The insurance agent sold me a $50,000 term life insurance policy.

ACTIVITY

Place commas where needed.

1. Would you mind George if we borrowed your picnic cooler this weekend?
2. The enchiladas served at Los Amigos 5607 Pacific Boulevard are the best in town.
3. An estimated 875000 African American men participated in the Million Man March on Washington on October 16 1995.
4. The mileage chart shows Elaine that we'll have to drive 1231 miles to get to Sarasota Florida.
5. The coupon refund address is 2120 Industrial Highway Great Plains Minnesota 55455.

Handbook of Sentence Skills

 Review Test 1

Insert commas where needed. In the space provided below each sentence, summarize briefly the rule that explains the comma or commas used.

1. "Kleenex tissues" said the history professor "were first used as gas mask filters in World War I."

   _____

2. Dee ordered a sundae with three scoops of vanilla ice cream miniature marsh-mallows and raspberry sauce.

   _____

3. While waiting to enter the movie theater we studied the faces of the people just leaving to see if they had liked the show.

   _____

4. I had left my wallet on the store counter but the clerk called me at home to say that it was safe.

   _____

5. The demonstrators protesting nuclear arms carried signs reading "Humans have never invented a weapon that they haven't used."

   _____

6. Large cactus plants which now sell for very high prices are being stolen from national parks and protected desert areas.

   _____

7. At the age of twenty-one Tiger Woods won the 1997 Masters Tournament with the highest margin of victory in the golfing tournament's history.

   _____

8. The talk-show guest a former child star said that one director threatened to shoot her dog if she didn't cry on cue.

   _____

9. Tom watched nervously as the dentist assembled drills mirrors clamps picks and cylinders of cotton on a tray next to the reclining chair.

   _____

10. Cats and dogs like most animals love the taste of salt and will lick humans' hands to get it.

    _____

■ **Review Test 2**

Insert commas where needed. Mark the one sentence that is correct with a C.

1. Before leaving for the gym Nikki added extra socks and a tube of shampoo to the gear in her duffel bag.

2. My father said "Golf isn't for me. I can't afford to buy lots of expensive sticks so that I can lose lots of expensive white balls."

3. Clogged with soggy birds' nests the chimney had allowed dangerous gases to accumulate in our house.

4. Oscar took a time-exposure photo of the busy highway so the cars' taillights appeared in the developed print as winding red ribbons.

5. On May 16 2003 my older brother got married and exactly a year later he got divorced.

6. During the summer graduation ceremony students fanned themselves with commencement programs and parents hid in the shade of trees.

7. Leaving eight astronauts dead the space shuttle *Columbia* broke apart as it returned to Earth on February 1 2003.

8. "When I was little" said Ernie "my brother told me it was illegal to kill praying mantises. I still don't know if that's true or not."

9. A huge side of beef its red flesh marbled with streaks of creamy fat hung from a razor-sharp steel hook.

10. A line of dancing numerals on *Sesame Street* kicked across the screen like a chorus line.

■ **Review Test 3**

In the following passage, there are ten missing commas. Add the commas where needed. The types of mistakes to look for are shown in the box below.

> 2 commas missing between items in a series
> 1 comma missing after introductory material
> 4 commas missing around interrupting words
> 2 commas missing between complete thoughts
> 1 comma missing with a direct quotation

Handbook of Sentence Skills

When I was about ten years old I developed several schemes to avoid eating liver, a food I despise. My first scheme involved my little brother. Timmy too young to realize what a horrible food liver is always ate every bit of his portion. On liver nights, I used to sit next to Tim and slide my slab of meat onto his plate when my parents weren't paying attention. This strategy worked until older and wiser Tim decided to reject his liver along with the rest of us. Another liver-disposal method I used was hiding the meat right on the plate. I'd cut the liver into tiny squares half the size of postage stamps and then I would carefully hide the pieces. I'd put them inside the skin of my baked potato beneath some mashed peas, or under a crumpled paper napkin. This strategy worked perfectly only if my mother didn't look too closely as she scraped the dishes. Once she said to me "Do you know you left a lot of liver on your plate?" My best liver trick was to hide the disgusting stuff on a three-inch-wide wooden ledge that ran under our dining-room table. I'd put little pieces of liver on the ledge when Mom wasn't looking; I would sneak the dried-up scraps into the garbage early the next day. Our dog would sometimes smell the liver try to get at it, and bang his head noisily against the bottom of the table. These strategies seemed like a lot of work but I never hesitated to take whatever steps I could. Anything was better than eating a piece of meat that tasted like old socks soaked in mud.

■ Review Test 4

On separate paper, write six sentences, one illustrating each of the six main comma rules.

40 Other Punctuation Marks

Colon (:)

24.2

Use the colon at the end of a complete statement to introduce a list, a long quotation, or an explanation.

1   List:

The store will close at noon on the following dates: November 26, December 24, and December 31.

2   Quotation:

In his book *Life Lines,* Forrest Church maintains that people should cry more: "Life is difficult. Some people pretend that it is not, that we should be able to breeze through. Yet hardly a week passes in which most of us don't have something worth crying about."

3   Explanation:

Here's a temporary solution to a dripping faucet: tie a string to it, and let the drops slide down the string to the sink.

ACTIVITY

Place colons where needed in the sentences below:

1. Bring these items to registration a ballpoint pen, your student ID card, and a check made out to the college.
2. The road was closed because of an emergency an enormous tree had fallen and blocked both lanes.

3. Willa Cather, the American author, had an insightful comment about plots "There are only two or three human stories, and they go on repeating themselves as fiercely as if they had never happened before."

Semicolon (;)

The main use of the semicolon is to mark a break between two complete thoughts, as explained on pages 436–439. Another use is to mark off items in a series when the items themselves contain commas. Here are some examples:

> Maya's children are named Melantha, which means "black flower"; Yonina, which means "dove"; and Cynthia, which means "moon goddess."

> My parents' favorite albums are *Rubber Soul,* by the Beatles; *Songs in the Key of Life,* by Stevie Wonder; and *Bridge over Troubled Water,* by Simon and Garfunkel.

ACTIVITY

Place semicolons where needed in the sentences below.

1. Strange things happen at very low temperatures a rose will shatter like glass.
2. My sister had a profitable summer: by mowing lawns, she earned $125 by washing cars, $85 and by walking the neighbors' dogs, $110.
3. The children who starred in the play were Kari Rosoff, nine years old Flora Junco, twelve years old and Ezra Johnson, three years old.

Dash (—)

A dash signals a pause longer than a comma but not as complete as a period. Use a dash to set off words for dramatic effect:

> I was so exhausted that I fell asleep within seconds—standing up.

> He had many good qualities—sincerity, honesty, and thoughtfulness—yet he had few friends.

> The pardon from the governor finally arrived—too late.

Notes

a A dash can be formed on a keyboard by striking the hyphen twice (--). Computer software also has a symbol for the dash. In handwriting, a dash is as long as two letters would be.

b Be careful not to overuse dashes.

ACTIVITY

Place dashes where needed in the following sentences.

1. The victim's leg broken in three places lay twisted at an odd angle on the pavement.
2. The wallet was found in a trash can minus the cash.
3. After nine days of hiking in the wilderness, sleeping under the stars, and communing with nature, I could think of only one thing a hot shower.

Parentheses ( )

ALLWRITE!
24.5

Parentheses are used to set off extra or incidental information from the rest of a sentence:

In 1913, the tax on an annual income of $4,000 (a comfortable wage at that time) was one penny.

Arthur C. Clarke, author of science fiction books (including *2001: A Space Odyssey*), was inspired as a young man by the magazine *Astounding Stories*.

Note   Do not use parentheses too often in your writing.

ACTIVITY

Add parentheses where needed.

1. Though the first *Star Trek* series originally ran for only three seasons 1965–1968, it gave rise to a number of spinoff shows which remain popular to this day.
2. Whenever Jack has too much to drink even one drink is sometimes too much, he becomes loud and abusive.
3. When I opened the textbook, I discovered that many pages mostly in the first chapter were completely blank.

Hyphen (-)

26.2

1   Use a hyphen with two or more words that act as a single unit describing a noun.

The light-footed burglar silently slipped open the sliding glass door.

While being interviewed on the late-night talk show, the quarterback announced his intention to retire.

With a needle, Rich punctured the fluid-filled blister on his toe.

2   Use a hyphen to divide a word at the end of a line of writing or typing. When you need to divide a word at the end of a line, divide it between syllables. Use your dictionary to be sure of correct syllable divisions.

Selena's first year at college was a time filled with numerous new pres-sures and responsibilities.

Notes

a   Do not divide words of one syllable.

b   Do not divide a word if you can avoid dividing it.

ACTIVITY

Place hyphens where needed.

1. The blood red moon hanging low on the horizon made a picture-perfect atmosphere for Halloween night.

2. My father, who grew up in a poverty stricken household, remembers putting cardboard in his shoes when the soles wore out.

3. The well written article in *Newsweek* described the nerve racking experiences of a journalist who infiltrated the mob.

■ Review Test

At the appropriate spot, place the punctuation mark shown in the margin.

—

1. A bad case of flu, a burglary, the death of an uncle it was not what you would call a pleasant week.

( ) 2. My grandfather who will be ninety in May says that hard work and a glass of wine every day are the secrets of a long life.

: 3. Mark Twain offered this advice to writers "The difference between the right word and the nearly right word is the difference between lightning and the lightning bug."

- 4. The passengers in the glass bottomed boat stared at the colorful fish in the water below.

( ) 5. Ellen's birthday December 27 falls so close to Christmas that she gets only one set of presents.

; 6. The dog-show winners included Freckles, a springer spaniel King Leo, a German shepherd and Big Guy, a miniature schnauzer.

— 7. I feel I have two chances of winning the lottery slim and none.

- 8. Cold hearted stepmothers are a fixture in many famous fairy tales.

; 9. Some people need absolute quiet in order to study they can't concentrate with the soft sounds of a radio, air conditioner, or television in the background.

: 10. A critic reviewing a bad play wrote, "I saw the play under the worst possible circumstances the curtain was up."

Word Use

41 Spelling Improvement

Poor spelling often results from bad habits developed in the early school years. With work, such habits can be corrected. If you can write your name without misspelling it, there is no reason why you cannot do the same with almost any word in the English language. Following are steps you can take to improve your spelling.

Step 1: Use the Dictionary

Get into the habit of using the dictionary. When you write a paper, allow yourself time to look up the spelling of all those words you are unsure about. Do not overlook the value of this step just because it is such a simple one. By using the dictionary, you can probably make yourself a 95 percent better speller.

Step 2: Keep a Personal Spelling List

Keep a list of words you misspell and study the words regularly. Write the list on the back page of a frequently used notebook or on a separate sheet of paper titled "Personal Spelling List."

To master the words on your personal spelling list, do the following:

1 Write down any hint that will help you remember the spelling of a word. For example, you might want to note that *occasion* is spelled with two *c*'s or that *all right* is two words, not one word.

2 Study a word by looking at it, saying it, and spelling it. You may also want to write out the word one or more times, or "air write" it with your finger in large, exaggerated motions.

3 When you have trouble spelling a long word, try to break the word into syllables and see whether you can spell the syllables. For example, *inadvertent* can be spelled easily if you can hear and spell in turn its four syllables: *in ad ver tent*. The word *consternation* can be spelled easily if you hear and spell its four

Spelling Improvement

syllables in turn: *con ster na tion*. Remember, then: Try to see, hear, and spell long words in terms of their syllables.

4   Keep in mind that review and repeated self-testing are keys to effective learning. When you are learning a series of words, go back after studying each new word and review all the preceding ones.

Step 3: Master Commonly Confused Words

Master the meanings and spellings of the commonly confused words on pages 535–543. Your instructor may assign twenty words for you to study at a time and give you a series of quizzes until you have mastered the words.

Step 4: Learn Key Words in Major Subjects

Make up and master lists of words central to the vocabulary of your major subjects. For example, a list of key words in business might include *economics, management, resources, scarcity, capitalism, decentralization, productivity, enterprise,* and so on; in psychology, *behavior, investigation, experimentation, frustration, cognition, stimulus, response, organism,* and so on. Set aside a specific portion of your various course notebooks to be used only for such lists, and study them using the methods described above for learning words.

Step 5: Study a Basic Word List

 Following is a list of 250 English words that are often misspelled. Study their spellings. Your instructor may assign 25 or 50 words for you to study at a time and give you a series of quizzes until you have mastered the entire list.

Handbook of Sentence Skills

250 Basic
Words

absence	comfortable	harass
ache	committed	height
achieve	completely	hospital
acknowledge	conceit	hundred
advice	conscience	husband
aisle	conscious	imitation
all right	conversation	incredible
already	cruelty	independent
amateur	50 daughter	instant
answer	deceit	instead
anxious	definite	intelligence
appearance	deposit	interest
appetite	dictionary	interfere
attempt	disastrous	interrupt
attendance	disease	irresistible
autumn	distance	January
awful	doctor	kindergarten
bachelor	doubt	100 leisure
balance	efficient	library
bargain	eighth	lightning
basically	either	likely
beautiful	emphasize	livelihood
believe	entrance	loneliness
beneficial	environment	loose
25 bottom	exaggerate	magazine
breathe	examine	making
brilliant	existence	maintain
bureau	familiar	marriage
business	fascinate	material
cafeteria	February	mathematics
calendar	financial	medicine
candidate	foreign	minute
category	forty	mortgage
ceiling	75 friend	muscle
cemetery	furniture	naturally
chief	government	necessary
choose	grammar	neither
cigarette	grieve	nickel
citizen	guidance	niece
college	hammer	ninety
column	handkerchief	noise

128

obedience	relieve	tournament
125 obstacle	religion	toward
occasion	representative	transferred
occur	resistance	trousers
occurrence	restaurant	truly
omission	rhythm	twelfth
opinion	ridiculous	unanimous
opportunity	right	until
optimist	175 safety	unusual
ounce	said	usage
outrageous	salary	used
pageant	scarcely	usual
pamphlet	scholastic	usually
people	science	vacuum
perform	scissors	valuable
persistent	secretary	variety
physically	seize	225 vegetable
picnic	separate	vengeance
plausible	sergeant	view
pleasant	several	villain
policeman	severely	vision
possible	shriek	visitor
precede	siege	voice
prefer	similar	Washington
preference	sincerely	wear
prejudice	sophomore	weather
150 prescription	straight	Wednesday
probably	succeed	weight
psychology	suppress	weird
pursue	telephone	welcome
quantity	temperature	whether
quarter	tenant	which
quiet	tendency	woman
quiz	200 tenth	women
raise	than	won't
really	theater	writing
recede	though	written
receive	thousand	wrong
recognize	through	yesterday
recommend	tomorrow	yolk
reference	tongue	your
region	tonight	250 you're
reign		

Step 6: Use Electronic Aids

There are several electronic aids that can help your spelling. First, most *electronic typewriters* can be set to beep automatically when you misspell a word. They include built-in dictionaries that will then give you the correct spelling. Second, *electronic spell-checks* are pocket-size devices that look much like the pocket calculators you may use in math class. Electronic spellers can be found in almost any electronics store. The checker includes a tiny keyboard. You type out the word the way you think it is spelled, and the checker quickly provides you with the correct spelling of related words. Finally, *a computer with a spell-checker* as part of its word-processing program will identify incorrect words and suggest correct spellings. If you know how to write on the computer, you will have little trouble learning how to use the spell-check feature.

42 Commonly Confused Words

Homonyms

Some words are commonly confused because they have the same sounds but different meanings and spellings; such words are known as *homonyms*. Following are a number of homonyms. Complete the activity for each set of words, and check off and study the words that give you trouble.

all ready   completely prepared
already   previously; before

It was *already* four o'clock by the time I thought about lunch.
My report was *all ready,* but the class was canceled.

Fill in the blanks: Tyrone was _____ to sign up for the course when he discovered that it had _____ closed.

brake   stop
break   come apart

The mechanic advised me to add *brake* fluid to my car.
During a commercial *break,* Marie lay on the floor and did fifty sit-ups.

Fill in the blanks: Tim, a poor driver, would always _____ at the last minute and would usually _____ the speed limit as well.

Handbook of Sentence Skills

course   part of a meal; a school subject; direction
coarse   rough

> At the movies, I tried to decide on a *course* of action that would put an end to the *coarse* language of the man behind me.

Fill in the blanks: Over the _____ of time, jagged, _____ rocks will be polished to smoothness by the pounding waves.

hear   perceive with the ear
here   in this place

> I can *hear* the performers so well from *here* that I don't want to change my seat.

Fill in the blanks: The chairperson explained that the meeting was being held _____ in the auditorium to enable everyone to _____ the debate.

hole   an empty spot
whole   entire

> A *hole* in the crumbling brick mortar made a convenient home for a small bird and its *whole* family.

Fill in the blanks: The _____ in Dave's argument wouldn't exist if he put his _____ concentration into his thinking.

its   belonging to it
it's   shortened form of "it is" or "it has"

> The tall giraffe lowered *its* head (the head belonging to the giraffe) to the level of the car window and peered in at us.
> *It's* (it is) too late to sign up for the theater trip to New York.

Fill in the blanks: I decided not to take the course because _____ too easy; _____ content offers no challenge whatever.

Commonly Confused Words

knew   past form of *know*
new   not old

No one *knew* our *new* phone number, but the obscene calls continued.

Fill in the blanks: Even people who _____ Charlie well didn't recognize him with his _____ beard.

know   to understand
no   a negative

By the time students complete that course, they *know* two computer languages and have *no* trouble writing their own programs.

Fill in the blanks: Dogs and cats usually _____ by the tone of the speaker's voice when they are being told "_____."

passed   went by; succeeded in; handed to
past   a time before the present; by, as in "I drove past the house"

As Yvonne *passed* exit six on the interstate, she knew she had gone *past* the correct turnoff.

Fill in the blanks: Lewis asked for a meeting with his boss to learn why he had been _____ over for promotion twice in the _____ year.

peace   calm
piece   a part

The best *piece* of advice she ever received was to maintain her own inner *peace.*

Fill in the blanks: Upon hearing that _____ of music, my angry mood was gradually replaced by one of _____.

plain   simple
plane   aircraft

The *plain* box contained a very expensive model *plane* kit.

Fill in the blanks: After unsuccessfully trying to overcome her fear, Selena finally admitted the _____ truth: she was terrified of flying in a _____.

principal   main; a person in charge of a school
principle   a law or standard

If the *principal* ingredient in this stew is octopus, I'll abandon my *principle* of trying everything at least once.

Fill in the blanks: Our _____ insists that all students adhere to every school _____ regarding dress, tardiness, and smoking.

right   correct; opposite of "left"
write   to put words on paper

Without the *right* amount of advance planning, it is difficult to *write* a good research paper.

Fill in the blanks: Connie wanted to send for the CDs offered on TV, but she could not _____ fast enough to get all the _____ information down before the commercial ended.

than   (thăn)   used in comparisons
then   (thĕn)   at that time

I made more money *then,* but I've never been happier *than* I am now.

Fill in the blanks: When I was in high school, I wanted a racy two-seater convertible more _____ anything else; but _____ my friends pointed out that only one person would be able to ride with me.

Commonly Confused Words

their	belonging to them
there	at that place; a neutral word used with verbs like *is, are, was, were, have,* and *had*
they're	shortened form of "they are"

The tenants *there* are complaining because *they're* being cheated by *their* landlord.

Fill in the blanks: The tomatoes I planted _____ in the back of the garden are finally ripening, but _____ bright red color will attract hungry raccoons, and I fear _____ going to be eaten.

| threw | past form of *throw* |
| through | from one side to the other; finished |

As the inexperienced pizza-maker *threw* the pie into the air, he punched a hole *through* its thin crust.

Fill in the blanks: As the president moved slowly _____ the cheering crowd, the Secret Service agent suddenly _____ himself at a man waving a small metal object.

to	verb part, as in *to smile;* toward, as in "I'm going *to* heaven"
too	overly, as in "The pizza was *too* hot"; also, as in "The coffee was hot, *too.*"
two	the number 2

I ran *to* the car *to* roll up the windows. (The first *to* means "toward"; the second *to* is a verb part that goes with *roll.*)

That amusement park is *too* far away; I hear that it's expensive, *too.* (The first *too* means "overly"; the second *too* means "also.")

The *two* players (2 players) jumped up to tap the basketball away.

Fill in the blanks: The _____ of them have been dating for a year, but lately they seem _____ be arguing _____ often to pretend nothing is wrong.

Handbook of Sentence Skills

wear   to have on
where   in what place

   Where I will *wear* a purple feather boa is not the point; I just want to buy it.

Fill in the blanks: _____ were we going the night I refused to _____ a tie?

weather   atmospheric conditions
whether   if it happens that; in case; if

   Although meteorologists are *weather* specialists, even they can't predict *whether* a hurricane will change course.

Fill in the blanks: The gloomy _____ report in the paper this morning ended all discussion of _____ to pack a picnic lunch for later.

whose   belonging to whom
who's   shortened form of "who is" and "who has"

   "*Who's* the patient *whose* filling fell out?" the dentist's assistant asked.

Fill in the blanks: _____ the salesperson _____ customers are always complaining about his high-pressure tactics?

your   belonging to you
you're   shortened form of "you are"

   You're making a fool of yourself; *your* Elvis imitation isn't funny.

Fill in the blanks: If _____ having trouble filling out _____ tax return, why don't you call the IRS's toll-free hot line?

Other Words Frequently Confused

21.6

Not all frequently confused words are homonyms. Here is a list of other words that people often confuse. Complete the activities for each set of words, and check off and study the words that give you trouble.

a
an

Both *a* and *an* are used before other words to mean, approximately, "one."

Generally you should use *an* before words starting with a vowel (*a, e, i, o, u*):

   an orange   an umbrella   an indication   an ape   an effort

Generally you should use *a* before words starting with a consonant (all other letters):

   a genius   a movie   a speech   a study   a typewriter

Fill in the blanks: The morning after the party, I had _____ pounding headache and _____ upset stomach.

accept   (ăk sĕpt′)   to receive; agree to
except   (ĕk sĕpt′)   excluding; but

   It was easy to *accept* the book's plot, *except* for one unlikely coincidence at the very end.

Fill in the blanks: Ved would _____ the position, _____ that it would add twenty minutes to his daily commute.

advice   (ăd vīs′)   noun meaning "an opinion"
advise   (ăd vīz′)   verb meaning "to counsel, to give advice"

   I have learned not to take my sister's *advice* on straightening out my life.
   A counselor can *advise* you about the courses you'll need next year.

Fill in the blanks: Karen is so troubled about losing her job that I will _____ her to seek the _____ of a professional counselor.

Handbook of Sentence Skills

affect   (uh fĕkt′)   verb meaning "to influence"
effect   (ĭ fĕkt′)   verb meaning "to cause something"; noun meaning "result"

> The bad weather will definitely *affect* the outcome of the election.
> If we can *effect* a change in George's attitude, he may do better in his courses.
> One *effect* of the strike will be dwindling supplies in the supermarkets.

Fill in the blanks: Scientists have studied the _____ of large quantities of saccharine on lab animals but have yet to learn how similar amounts

_____ human beings.

among   implies three or more
between   implies only two

> After the team of surgeons consulted *among* themselves, they decided that the bullet was lodged *between* two of the patient's ribs.

Fill in the blanks: _____ halves, one enthusiastic fan stood up

_____ his equally fanatic friends and took off his coat and shirt.

beside   along the side of
besides   in addition to

> *Besides* doing daily inventories, I have to stand *beside* the cashier whenever the store gets crowded.

Fill in the blanks: _____ those books on the table, I plan to use these

magazines stacked _____ me while doing my research paper.

fewer   used with things that can be counted
less   refers to amount, value, or degree

> I've taken *fewer* classes this semester, so I hope to have *less* trouble finding time to study.

Fill in the blanks: This beer advertises that it has _____ calories and

is _____ filling.

former   refers to the first of two items named
latter   refers to the second of two items named

Sue yelled at her sons, Greg and John, when she got home; the *former* (Greg) had left the refrigerator open and the *latter* (John) had left wet towels all over the bathroom.

Fill in the blanks: Eddy collects coupons and parking tickets: the _____

save him money and the _____ are going to cost him a great deal of money some day.

learn   to gain knowledge
teach   to give knowledge

I can't *learn* a new skill unless someone with lots of patience *teaches* me.

Fill in the blanks: Because she is quick to _____ new things, Mandy

has offered to _____ me how to play the latest video games.

loose   (lo͞os)   not fastened; not tight-fitting
lose   (lo͞oz)   to misplace; fail to win

In this strong wind, the house may *lose* some of its *loose* roof shingles.

Fill in the blanks: A _____ wire in the television set was causing us

to _____ the picture.

quiet   (kwī′ĭt)   peaceful
quite   (kwīt)   entirely; really; rather

Jennifer seems *quiet* and demure, but she has *quite* a temper at times.

Fill in the blanks: Most people think the library is _____ a good

place to study, but I find the extreme _____ distracting.

Handbook of Sentence Skills

ACTIVITY

These sentences check your understanding of *its, it's; there, their, they're; to, too, two;* and *your, you're.* Underline the two incorrect spellings in each sentence. Then spell the words correctly in the spaces provided.

_____ 1. "Its not a very good idea," yelled Alexandra's boss, "to tell you're customer
_____   that the striped dress she plans to buy makes her look like a pregnant tiger."

_____ 2. You're long skirt got stuck in the car door, and now its sweeping the highway.

_____ 3. When your young, their is a tendency to confuse a crush with true love.

_____ 4. After too hours of typing, Lin was to tired to type any longer.

_____ 5. It is unusual for a restaurant to lose it's license, but this one had more mice
_____   in its' kitchen than cooks.

_____ 6. The vampires bought a knife sharpener in order too sharpen there teeth.

_____ 7. Your sometimes surprised by who you're friends turn out to be in difficult
_____   times.

_____ 8. When the children get to quiet, Clare knows their getting into trouble.

_____ 9. There friendship developed into love as the years passed, and now, in midlife,
_____   their newlyweds.

_____ 10. There is no reason to panic if you get a bad grade or too. Its well known that
_____   many successful people were not great students.

Review Test 1

Underline the correct word in the parentheses. Rather than guessing, look back at the explanations of the words when necessary.

1. I (know, no) that several of the tenants have decided (to, too, two) take (their, there, they're) case to court.

Commonly Confused Words

2. (Whose, Who's) the author of that book about the (affects, effects) of eating (to, too, two) much protein?

3. In our supermarket is a counter (where, wear) (your, you're) welcome to sit down and have free coffee and doughnuts.

4. (Its, It's) possible to (loose, lose) friends by constantly giving out unwanted (advice, advise).

5. For a long time, I couldn't (accept, except) the fact that my husband wanted a divorce; (then, than) I decided to stop being angry and get on with life.

6. I spent the (hole, whole) day browsing (threw, through) the chapters in my business textbook, but I didn't really study them.

7. The newly appointed (principal, principle) is (quite, quiet) familiar with the problems (hear, here) at our school.

8. I found that our cat had (all ready, already) had her kittens (among, between) the weeds (beside, besides) the porch.

9. I (advice, advise) you not to take children to that movie; the special (affects, effects) are (to, too, two) frightening.

10. It seems that nobody will ever be able to (learn, teach) Mario to take (fewer, less) chances with his car.

Review Test 2

On separate paper, write short sentences using the ten words shown below.

1. accept

2. its

3. you're

4. too

5. then

6. principal

7. their

8. passed

9. fewer

10. who's

43 Effective Word Choice

Choose your words carefully when you write. Always take the time to think about your word choices rather than simply use the first word that comes to mind. You want to develop the habit of selecting words that are precise and appropriate for your purpose. One way you can show sensitivity to language is by avoiding slang, clichés, and pretentious words.

Slang

21.3a

We often use slang expressions when we talk because they are so vivid and colorful. However, slang is usually out of place in formal writing. Here are some examples of slang:

Someone *ripped off* Ken's new Adidas running shoes from his locker.

After the game, we *stuffed our faces* at the diner.

I finally told my parents to *get off my case.*

The movie really *grossed me out.*

Slang expressions have a number of drawbacks. They go out of date quickly, they become tiresome if used excessively in writing, and they may communicate clearly to some readers but not to others. Also, the use of slang can be an evasion of the specific details that are often needed to make one's meaning clear in writing. For example, in "The movie really grossed me out," the writer has not provided the specific details about the movie necessary for us to clearly understand the statement. Was it acting, special effects, or violent scenes that the writer found so disgusting? In general, then, you should avoid slang in your writing. If you are in doubt about whether an expression is slang, it may help to check a recently published hardbound dictionary.

Effective Word Choice

ACTIVITY

Rewrite the following sentences, replacing the italicized slang words with more formal ones.

EXAMPLE When we told the neighbors to *can the noise,* they *freaked out.*

When we told the neighbors to be quiet, they got upset.

1. I didn't realize how *messed up* Joey was until he stole some money from his parents and *split* for a month.

   _____

   _____

   _____

2. Greg was so *bummed out* the day he got fired that he didn't do anything except *veg out* in front of the TV.

   _____

   _____

   _____

3. Theo was so *wiped out* after his workout at the gym that he couldn't *get it together* to defrost a frozen dinner.

   _____

   _____

   _____

4. When Rick tried to *put the move on* Lola at the school party, she told him to *shove off.*

   _____

   _____

   _____

5. The entire town was *psyched* that the corrupt mayor *got busted.*

   _____

   _____

   _____

Clichés

21.5

A *cliché* is an expression that has been worn out through constant use. Here are some typical clichés:

short but sweet	last but not least
drop in the bucket	work like a dog
had a hard time of it	all work and no play
word to the wise	it goes without saying
it dawned on me	at a loss for words
sigh of relief	taking a big chance
too little, too late	took a turn for the worse
singing the blues	easier said than done
in the nick of time	on top of the world
too close for comfort	time and time again
saw the light	make ends meet

Clichés are common in speech but make your writing seem tired and stale. Also, they are often an evasion of the specific details that you must work to provide in your writing. You should, then, avoid clichés and try to express your meaning in fresh, original ways.

ACTIVITY 1

Underline the cliché in each of the following sentences. Then substitute specific, fresh words for the trite expression.

EXAMPLE My boyfriend has stuck with me through thick and thin.

through good times and bad

1. As the only girl in an otherwise all-boy family, I got away with murder.

_____

Effective Word Choice

2. When I realized I'd lost my textbook, I knew I was up the creek without a paddle.

_____

3. My suggestion is just a shot in the dark, but it's better than nothing.

_____

4. Janice got more than she bargained for when she offered to help Larry with his math homework.

_____

5. Bob is pushing his luck by driving a car with bald tires.

_____

6. On a hot, sticky midsummer day, iced tea or any frosty drink really hits the spot.

_____

7. Nadia thanks her lucky stars that she was born with brains, beauty, and humility.

_____

8. Anything that involves mathematical ability has always been right up my alley.

_____

9. Your chance of buying a good used car from that dealer is one in a million.

_____

10. Even when we are up to our eyeballs in work, our boss wonders if we have enough to do.

_____

ACTIVITY 2

Write a short paragraph describing the kind of day you had. Try to put as many clichés as possible into it. For example, "I got up at the crack of dawn, ready to take on the world. I grabbed a bite to eat. . . ." By making yourself aware of clichés in this way, you should lessen the chance that they will appear in your writing.

Pretentious Words

Some people feel that they can improve their writing by using fancy, elevated words rather than simple, natural words. They use artificial, stilted language that more often obscures their meaning than communicates it clearly. Here are some unnatural-sounding sentences:

It was a splendid opportunity to get some slumber.

We relished the delicious repast.

The officer apprehended the intoxicated operator of the vehicle.

This establishment sells women's apparel and children's garments.

The same thoughts can be expressed more clearly and effectively by using plain, natural language, as below:

It was a good chance to get some sleep.

We enjoyed the delicious meal.

The officer arrested the drunken driver.

This store sells women's and children's clothes.

Here are some other inflated words and simpler words that could replace them:

Inflated Words	Simpler Words
subsequent to	after
finalize	finish
transmit	send
facilitate	help
component	part
initiate	begin
delineate	describe
manifested	shown
to endeavor	to try

Effective Word Choice

ACTIVITY

Cross out the inflated words in each sentence. Then substitute clear, simple language for the inflated words.

EXAMPLE The ~~conflagration~~ was ~~initiated~~ by an arsonist.

The fire was started by an arsonist.

1. Rico and his brother do not interrelate in a harmonious manner.

_____

2. The meaning of the movie's conclusion eluded my comprehension.

_____

3. The departmental conference will commence promptly at two o'clock.

_____

4. A man dressed in odd attire accosted me on the street.

_____

5. When my writing implement malfunctioned, I asked the professor for another.

_____

■ Review Test

Certain words are italicized in the following sentences. In the space provided at the left, identify the words as slang (S), a cliché (C), or pretentious words (PW). Then replace the words with more effective diction.

_____ 1. Losing weight is *easier said than done* for someone who loves sweets.

_____

_____ 2. After dinner, we washed the *culinary utensils* and wrapped the *excess* food.

_____

_____ 3. Bruce is so stubborn that talking to him is like *talking to a brick wall.*

_____

_____ 4. Michelle spent the summer *watching the tube* and *catching rays.*

_____

_____ 5. The fans, *all fired up* after the game, *peeled out* of the parking lot and honked their horns.

_____

Handbook of Sentence Skills

_____ 6. The stew I made contained *everything but the kitchen sink.*

_____ 7. That *guy* isn't really a criminal; he's just gotten a *bum rap.*

_____ 8. A company cannot *implement changes and attain growth* without *input from its personnel.*

_____ 9. I failed the test, and to *add insult to injury,* I got a low grade on my paper.

_____ 10. I *perused* several *periodicals* while I waited for the doctor.

Take the whole range of imaginative literature, and we are all wholesale borrowers. In every matter that relates to invention, to use, or beauty or form, we are borrowers.

—WENDELL PHILLIPS

APA
Documentation
Style

7 APA Documentation Style

APA IN-TEXT CITATIONS: DIRECTORY TO SAMPLE TYPES (CHAPTER 29)

(See pp. 250–58 for examples of references.)

APA REFERENCE ENTRIES: DIRECTORY TO SAMPLE TYPES (CHAPTER 30)

(See pp. 245–50 for examples of in-text citations.)

Books

Periodicals

Instructors of social science and professional courses in psychology, sociology, political science, communications, education, and business usually prefer a documentation style that emphasizes the author and the year of publication, in part because the style makes it easy to tell if the sources cited are current.

The American Psychological Association (APA) has developed a widely used version of the author-year style; the information in Chapters 29–31 is based on the fifth edition of its *Publication Manual* (Washington: APA, 2001).

APA documentation style has two mandatory parts:

- In-text citations
- List of references

For links to Web sites for documentation styles used in various disciplines, visit <www.mhhe.com/maimon/mla_documentation>.

29   APA Style: In-Text Citations

When you use ideas, information, or words from a source, APA in-text citation format requires that you do the following:

- **Identify the author(s) of the source,** either in the sentence or in a parenthetical citation.

TEXTCONNEX

FAQs on APA Style

For updates to the APA documentation system, check the APA-sponsored Web site at <http://www.apastyle.org>.

- **Indicate the year of publication of the source** following the author's name, either in parentheses if the author's name is part of the sentence or if the author is not named in the sentence, after the author's name and a comma in a parenthetical citation.

- **Include a page reference for a quotation or a specific piece of information.** Put a *p.* before the page number. If the author is named in the text, the page number appears in the parenthetical citation following the borrowed material. Page numbers are not necessary when you are summarizing the source as a whole or paraphrasing an idea found throughout a work. (*For more on summary, paraphrase, and quotation, see Tab 5: Researching, pp. 186–87.*)

1. Author named in your sentence: When the author is named in a signal phrase, follow the name with the year of publication (in parentheses).

    According to Eidson (1992), several political parties
    vie for power at every level during regularly
    scheduled elections.

2. Author named in parentheses: If you do not name the source's author in your sentence, then you must include the name in the parentheses, followed by the date and, if you are giving a quotation or a specific piece of information, the page number. The name, date, and page number are separated by commas.

    This safety net plus the free market comprise what
    Germany calls a "social market" economy (Eidson, 1992,
    p. 122).

LEARNING in COLLEGE

What Is the American Psychological Association?

The American Psychological Association (APA) is the largest psychological organization in the world. This scientific and professional group has more than 155,000 members and supports advances in psychological research and in the practice of psychology. Now in its fifth edition, the *Publication Manual of the American Psychological Association* has become an accepted guide for writers in many areas of science, not just psychology. Like the *MLA Handbook* (*see p. 204*), the *Publication Manual* is concerned with the mechanics of academic writing. The manual is especially useful in helping students prepare and present scientific facts and figures, and it contains special sections on how to construct tables, how to present statistics, and how to cite scientific references.

3. Two to five authors: If a source has five or fewer authors, name all of them the first time you cite the source.

> As Calhoun, Light, and Keller (1997) point out,
> "Income-based rankings are not necessarily a measure
> of development" (p. 468).

If you put the names of the authors in parentheses, use an ampersand (&) instead of *and*.

> Although income-based rankings are important, they
> "are not necessarily a measure of development"
> (Calhoun, Light, & Keller, 1997, p. 468).

After the first time you cite a work by three or more authors, use the first author's name plus *et al.* Always use both names when citing a work by two authors.

> Another key factor is income distribution within
> countries (Calhoun et al., 1997, p. 470).

4. Six or more authors: In all in-text citations of a work by six or more authors, give the first author's name plus *et al.* In the reference list, however, list the first six authors' names, followed by *et al.* for all others.

```
As Barbre et al. (1989) have argued, using personal

narratives enables researchers to connect the

individual and the social.
```

5. Organization as author: Treat the organization as the author and spell out its name the first time the source is cited. If the organization is well known, you may use an abbreviation thereafter.

```
The Deutsche Bank's Economics Department (1991)

identified a handful of key problems raised by

efforts to rebuild eastern Europe.
```

```
Public service announcements were used to inform

parents of these findings (National Institute of

Mental Health [NIMH], 1991).
```

In subsequent citations, as long as you are sure that readers will know what the abbreviation stands for, only the abbreviation and the date need to be given: *(NIMH, 1991)*.

6. Unknown author: When no author or editor is listed for a work, use the first one or two important words of the title. Use quotation marks for titles of articles or chapters and italics for titles of books or reports.

```
The transformation of women's lives has been hailed as

"the single most important change of the past 1,000

years" ("Reflections," 1999, p. 77).
```

7. Two or more authors with the same last name: If the authors of two or more sources have the same last name, always include the appropriate first initial, even when the year of publication differs.

```
M. Smith (1988) showed how globalization has

restructured both cities and states.
```

8. Two or more sources cited at one time: When you are indebted to two or more sources for an idea, cite the authors in the order in which they appear in the list of references. Separate the two sources with a semicolon.

During World War II, the Nazi regime developed an
agrarian ideology while accelerating the pace of
industrial growth (Eidson, 1992; "Germany," 1995).

9. E-mail, letters, conversations: To cite information received
from unpublished forms of personal communication, such as conversations, letters, notes, and e-mail messages, give the source's initials
and last name, and provide as precise a date as possible.

According to A. Tapolcai (personal communication,
April 3, 1996), college-educated Hungarians had long
expected this kind of change.

Note: Because readers do not have access to them, you should not
include personal communications—e-mail, notes, and letters—in your
reference list.

10. Indirect source: When referring to a source that you know only
from reading another source, use the phrase *as cited in,* followed by the
author of the source you actually read and its year of publication.

A study by Passell (as cited in Calhoun et al., 1997,
p. 469) found that investments in education and
technology were lower for countries that exported
natural resources.

Note: The work by Passell would not be included in the reference list,
but the work by Calhoun et al. would.

11. Electronic source: Cite an electronic source the same way you
would a print source, with the author's last name and the publication
date. If the document is a pdf (portable document format) file with sta-
ble page numbers, cite the page number as you would a print source.
If the source has paragraph numbers instead of page numbers, use
para. or ¶ instead of *p.* when citing a specific part of the source.

According to Gordeeva (2000), by the time the Truehand
was disbanded, it had privatized around 14,000
enterprises (para. 2).

Note: If the specific part lacks any kind of page or paragraph num-
bering, cite the heading and the number of the paragraph under
that heading where the information can be found. If you cannot find

the name of the author, or if the author is an organization, follow the appropriate guidelines for print sources (*see #5 and #6*). If you cannot determine the date, use the abbreviation "n.d." in its place: (*Wilson, n.d.*).

30   APA Style: References

APA documentation style requires a list of references where readers can find complete bibliographical information about the sources referred to in your paper. The list of references should appear at the end of your paper, beginning on a new page entitled "References."

Books

1. Book with one author:

```
Brown, J. F. (1991). Surge to freedom: The end of
        communist rule in eastern Europe. Durham, NC:
        Duke University Press.
```

2. Book with two or more authors:

```
Brown, L., Lenssen, N., & Kane, H. (1995). Vital signs
        1995: The trends that are shaping our future. New
        York: Norton.

Zelikow, P., & Rice, C. (1995). Germany unified and
        Europe transformed: A study in statecraft.
        Cambridge, MA: Harvard University Press.
```

3. Organization as author: To credit a subdivision like "Economics Department," put its name after the name of the parent organization. When the publisher is the same as the author, use the word "Author" instead of repeating the organization's name as the publisher.

```
Deutsche Bank, Economics Department. (1991). Rebuilding
        eastern Europe. Frankfurt, Germany: Author.
```

4. Two or more works by the same author: List the works in publication order, the earliest one first.

GENERAL GUIDELINES for the LIST of REFERENCES in APA STYLE

1. Begin on a new page.
2. Begin with the centered title "References."
3. Include a reference for every in-text citation.
4. Put references in alphabetical order by author's last name.
5. Give the last name and first or both initials for each author.
6. Put the publication year in parentheses following the author or authors' names.
7. Capitalize only the first word and proper nouns in titles. Also capitalize the first word following the semicolon in a subtitle.
8. Use italics for titles of books but not articles. Do not enclose titles of articles in quotation marks.
9. Include the city and publisher for books. If the city is not well known, include the state, using its two-letter postal abbreviation.
10. Include the periodical name and volume number (both in italics) as well as the page numbers for a periodical article.
11. Separate the author's or authors' names, date (in parentheses), title, and publication information with periods.
12. Use a hanging indent: Begin the first line of each entry flush left, and indent all subsequent lines of an entry one-half inch (five spaces).
13. Double-space within and between entries.

Brown, J. F. (1988). *Eastern Europe and communist rule.*
    Durham, NC: Duke University Press.

Brown, J. F. (1991). *Surge to freedom: The end of*
    communist rule in eastern Europe. Durham, NC:
    Duke University Press.

If the works were published in the same year, put them in alphabetical order by title and add a letter (*a, b, c*) to the year so that you can distinguish each entry in your in-text citations; see #15 for an example related to periodicals.

5. Book with editor(s): Add (*Ed.*) or (*Eds.*) after the name. If a book lists an author and an editor, treat the editor like a translator (*see #7*).

```
Stares, P. B. (Ed.). (1992). The new Germany and the

     new Europe. Washington, DC: Brookings Institution.
```

6. Selection in an edited book or anthology:
The selection's author, year of publication, and title come first, followed by the word *In* and information about the edited book. Note that the page numbers of the selection go in parentheses after the book's title.

```
Kreile, M. (1992). The political economy of the new

     Germany. In P. B. Stares (Ed.), The new Germany

     and the new Europe (pp. 55–92). Washington, DC:

     Brookings Institution.
```

7. Translation:
After the title of the translation, put the name(s) of the translator(s) in parentheses, followed by the abbreviation *Trans.*

```
Jarausch, K. H., & Gransow, V. (1994). Uniting

     Germany: Documents and debates, 1944–1993 (A.

     Brown & B. Cooper, Trans.). Providence, RI: Berg.
```

8. Article in a reference work:
Some encyclopedias and similar reference works name the authors of individual selections. Begin with the author's name, if given. If no author is given, begin with the title of the selection.

```
Eidson, J. R. (1992). Germans. In Encyclopedia of

     world cultures (Vol. 4, pp. 121–124). Boston:

     G. K. Hall.
```

9. Unknown author or editor:
Start with the title. When alphabetizing, use the first important word of the title (excluding articles such as *The, A,* or *An*).

```
Give me liberty. (1969). New York: World.
```

10. Edition other than the first:
After the title, put the edition number in parentheses, followed by a period.

```
Smyser, W. R. (1993). The German economy: Colossus at

     crossroads (2nd ed.). New York: St. Martin's

     Press.
```

11. One volume of a multivolume work: If the specific volume used has its own title, put it before the title of the whole work. Note that no period separates the parenthetical volume number and the title that precedes it.

```
Kintner, E. W. (Ed.). (1978). The Clayton Act and
    amendments. In The legislative history of the
    federal antitrust laws and related statutes:
    The antitrust laws (Vol. 2). New York: Chelsea
    House.
```

12. Republished book:

```
Le Bon, G. (1960). The crowd: A study of the popular
    mind. New York: Viking. (Original work published
    1895).
```

Note: In-text citations should give both years: "As Le Bon (1895/1960) pointed out. . . ."

Periodicals

13. Article in a journal paginated by volume: Do not put the article title in quotation marks, and do not use *pp.* before the page numbers. Italicize the title of the periodical and the volume number.

```
Arnold, E. (1991). German foreign policy and
    unification. International Affairs, 67, 483–491.
```

14. Article in a journal paginated by issue: Include the issue number (in parentheses). Notice that the issue number is not italicized as part of the journal's title.

```
Lowe, J. H., & Bargas, S. E. (1996). Direct investment
    positions and historical-cost basis. Survey of
    Current Business, 76(7), 45–60.
```

15. Two or more works in one year by the same author: Alphabetize the works by title, and attach a letter to each entry's year of publication, beginning with *a,* then *b,* and so on. In-text citations must use the letter as well as the year so that readers know exactly which work is being cited.

```
Agarwal, J. P. (1996a). Does foreign direct investment
    contribute to unemployment in home countries?—
    An empirical survey (Discussion Paper No. 765).
    Kiel, Germany: Institute of World Economics.

Agarwal, J. P. (1996b). Impact of Europe agreements on
    FDI in developing countries. International
    Journal of Social Economics, 23(10/11), 150–163.
```

Note: Also see #22, which explains the format for a report or working paper.

16. Article in a magazine: After the year, add the month for magazines published monthly or the month and day for magazines published weekly. Note that the volume number is also included, as it is for journals.

```
Klee, K. (1999, December 13). The siege of Seattle.
    Newsweek, 134, 30–35.
```

17. Article in a newspaper: Use *p.* or *pp.* with the section and page number. List all page numbers, separated by commas, if the article appears on discontinuous pages: *pp. C1, C4, C6.* If there is no identified author, begin with the title of the article.

```
Andrews, E. L. (1999, February 7). With German craft
    rules it's hard just to get work. The New York
    Times, p. A16.
```

18. Editorial or letter to the editor: In brackets, add to the title a phrase describing the form of the source.

```
Krugman, P. (2000, July 16). Who's acquiring whom?
    [Editorial]. The New York Times, Sec. 4, p. 15.
```

19. Unsigned article: Begin the entry with the title, and alphabetize it by the first important word (excluding articles such as *The, A,* or *An*).

```
Reflection on a thousand years: Introduction. (1999,
    April 18). The New York Times Magazine, p.77.
```

20. Review:

> Bontolft, G. J. (1992). Culture shock in east Germany.
> [Review of the book *Freedom was never like this:*
> *A winter's journey in east Germany*]. *Contemporary*
> *Review, 260,* 49–50.

Note: If the review is untitled, use the bracketed description in place of a title.

Other Print and Audiovisual Sources

21. Government document: When no author is listed, use the government agency as the author.

> U.S. House Committee on Small Business. (1990). *East*
> *Germany's time of crisis.* Washington, D.C.: U.S.
> Government Printing Office.

22. Report or working paper: If the issuing agency numbered the report, include that number in parentheses after the title.

> Agarwal, J. P. (1996a). *Does foreign direct investment*
> *contribute to unemployment in home countries?—An*
> *empirical survey* (Discussion Paper No. 765).
> Kiel, Germany: Institute of World Economics.

Note: For reports from a deposit service like the *Educational Resources Information Center (ERIC)*, put the document number in parentheses at the end of the entry.

23. Conference presentation: Treat published conference presentations as a selection in a book (*#6*), as a periodical article (*#13 or #14*), or as a report (*#22*), whichever applies. For unpublished conference presentations, including poster sessions, provide the author, the year and month of the conference, the title of the presentation, and information on the presentation's form, forum, and place.

> Markusen, J. (1998, June). *The role of multinationals*
> *in global economic analysis.* Paper presented at
> the First Annual Conference in Global Economic
> Analysis, West Lafayette, IN.

Desantis, R. (1998, June). *Optimal export taxes,*
welfare, industry concentration and firm size:
A general equilibrium analysis. Poster session
presented at the First Annual Conference in
Global Economic Analysis, West Lafayette, IN.

24. Unpublished dissertation or dissertation abstract:

Weinbaum, A. E. (1998). Genealogies of "race" and
reproduction in transatlantic modern thought
(Doctoral dissertation, Columbia University,
1998). *Dissertation Abstracts International,*
58, 229.

If you used the abstract but not the actual dissertation, treat the
entry like a periodical article, with *Dissertation Abstracts Interna-*
tional as the periodical.

Weinbaum, A. E. (1998). Genealogies of "race" and
reproduction in transatlantic modern thought.
Dissertation Abstracts International, 58, 229.

25. Film, videotape, recording: Begin with the cited person's
name and, if appropriate, a parenthetical notation of his or her role.
After the title, identify the medium in brackets, followed by the country and name of the distributor.

Towner, R. (1989). *City of eyes* [Record]. Munich: ECM.

Wenders, W. (Director). (1989). *Wings of desire*
[Videotape]. Germany: Orion Home Video.

26. Television program: When citing a single episode, treat the
script writer as the author and the producer as the editor of the
series.

Weissman, G. (Writer). (2000). Mississippi: River out
of control [Television series episode]. In J.
Towers (Producer), *Wrath of God.* New York: The
History Channel.

When citing a whole series or a specific news broadcast, name the producer as author.

```
Towers, J. (Producer). (2000). Wrath of God. New York:
     The History Channel.

Crystal, L. (Executive Producer). (2000, July 18). The
     NewsHour with Jim Lehrer [Television broadcast].
     Washington, D.C.: Public Broadcasting Service.
```

Electronic Sources

27. Online article or abstract from a database: When you use material from databases such as *PsycInfo, Sociological Abstracts, General BusinessFile ASAP,* and *Lexis-Nexis,* include a retrieval date and the name of the database in addition to the standard information about author, year, title, and publisher.

```
Waelde, T. W. (1996). International energy investment.
     Energy Law Journal, 17, 191-223. Retrieved May
     10, 2000, from Lexis-Nexis database.

Haas, R. (1994). Eastern Europe: A subsidy strategy
     for ecological recovery. Global Energy Issues
     6(3), 133-138. Abstract retrieved April 22, 2001,
     from Lexis-Nexis database.
```

Note: When citing an abstract instead of the article, add the word *abstract* to the retrieval statement.

28. Internet article: When citing an article from a journal that appears only online, include a retrieval date and the URL.

```
Leydesdorff, L., & Etzkowitz, H. (2001). The
     transformation of university-industry-government
     relations. Electronic Journal of Sociology 5.
     Retrieved December 10, 2001, from http://
     www.sociology.org/content/vol005.004/th.html
```

Note: To cite an electronic version of an article from a print journal, use the standard format for a periodical article (*see #13*) and add [*Electronic version*] after the article title.

APA

Tips

APA EXPLANATORY NOTES

APA discourages the use of explanatory content notes to supplement the ideas in your paper, but they *are* an option. If you decide it is necessary to include a few content notes, put superscript numbers at appropriate points in your text. Type the notes, double spaced, on a separate page with the centered title "Footnotes." Indent the first line of each note five spaces, and type the appropriate superscript number followed by the note, with all lines after the first flush with the left margin.

29. Document in a Web site:

```
Fisher, B. (1995). U.S. global trade outlook: Germany
     (Office of European Union and Regional Affairs
     Report). Retrieved November 7, 1997, from
     http://tradeport.org/ts/ntdb/usgto/selcoun.html

U.S. Department of State. (1997). Germany: Economic
     policy and trade practices, 1996. Retrieved
     November 7, 1997, from http://tradeport.org/ts/
     countries/germany.html
```

30. Online posting to news group, discussion forum, or mailing list:
Messages posted to archived online electronic mailing lists, discussion forums, or news groups can be retrieved and should therefore be included in the reference list when you use them as sources. Provide the message's author, its date, and the subject line as the title. After the phrase *Message posted to,* give the name of the discussion forum or news group, followed by the address of the message.

```
Red Wave. (2000, April 8). Pareto/allocative efficiency
     of gift economy. Message posted to alt.society.
     economic-dev message board, archived at http://
     www.remarq.com/read/9755/qAyjNymZ61SoC-vwH#LR
```

31. Computer software:

```
AllWrite! 3.0 with Online Handbook. (2003). [Computer
     software]. New York: McGraw-Hill.
```

31 APA Style: Paper Format

The following guidelines will help you prepare your research paper in the format recommended by the *Publication Manual of the American Psychological Association,* fifth edition. For an example of a research paper that has been prepared using APA style, see pages 261–72.

Materials. Before printing your paper, make sure that you have stored your final draft on a backup disk. Use a high-quality printer and good white 8½-by-11-inch paper. Choose a standard 10- or 12-point font such as Courier, Times, or Bookman. Do not justify your text or hyphenate words at the right margin; it should be ragged.

Title page. The first page of your paper should be a title page. Center the title between the left and right margins in the upper half of the page, and put your name a few lines below the title. Most instructors will also want you to include the course number and title, the instructor's name, and the date. (*See p. 261 for an example.*)

Margins and spacing. Use one-inch margins all around, except for the right-hand top corner, where the page number goes.

Double-space lines throughout the paper, including in the abstract, within any notes, and in the list of references. Indent the first word of each paragraph one-half inch (or five spaces).

For quotations of more than 40 words, use block format and indent five spaces from the left margin. Double-space the quoted lines.

Page numbers and abbreviated titles. All pages, including the title page, should have a number preceded by a short (one- or two-word) version of your title. Put this information in the upper right-hand corner of each page, about one-half inch from the top.

Abstract. Instructors sometimes require an abstract—a 75- to 100-word summary of your paper's thesis, major points or lines of development, and conclusions. The abstract appears on its own numbered page, entitled "Abstract," and is placed right after the title page. (*For more on abstracts, see Tab 3: Common Assignments across the Curriculum, p. 114.*)

Headings. Although headings are not required, most instructors of social science and professional courses welcome them. The primary headings should be centered, and all key words in the heading should be capitalized.

You can also use secondary headings if you need them; they should be italicized and should appear flush against the left-hand margin. Do not use a heading for your introduction, however. (*For more on headings, see Tab 9: Document and Web Design, pp. 318–19.*)

Visuals. Place visuals (tables, charts, graphs, and images) close to the place in your text where you refer to them. Label each visual as a table or a figure, and number each kind consecutively (Table 1, Table 2). You will also need to provide an informative caption for each visual. Cite the source of the material, preceded by the word *Note* and a period, and provide explanatory notes as needed. (*For more on using visuals effectively, see Tab 9: Document and Web Design, pp. 319–25.*)

To view another sample student paper written in APA style, visit <www.mhhe.com/maimon/apa_paper_format>.

32 Student Paper in APA Style

Jennifer Koehler researched and wrote the following report on Germany for a course entitled *Business in the Global Environment.* Because the most up-to-date business information was available on the World Wide Web, Jennifer consulted a number of online sources in addition to print sources.

Germany's Path   1

All pages:
short title and
page number.

Germany's Path to Continuing Prosperity

Jennifer L. Koehler

GLB301 Country Report

Business in the Global Environment

Professor Meznar

November 14, 1997

Full title,
centered.

Germany's Path   2

Abstract

With reunification, Germany faces a major economic challenge. With proper follow through, it can become one of the world's primary sources of direct investment and maintain its status as one of the world's preeminent exporters. The eastern area needs to be brought up to the western area's standards. Germany is as attractive a market for other nations and as a location for production because of its position at the crossroads of Europe. If government efforts continue, the economy will strengthen, and Germany will reinforce its position as a nation integral to the global economy.

First line is not indented.

Abstract summarizes main points of paper.

Paragraph should be no longer than 120 words.

1"   ½"

Germany's Path   3

Germany's Path to Continuing Prosperity

With reunification, Germany faces a major economic challenge. How might a society succeed in combining two completely different economies and cultures bound only by a common language? The German government stepped in to ease the reunification process, but the result was unfortunate: an expensive and intrusive bureaucracy drained Germany's resources and reduced its appeal for corporate investors. A sagging economy followed. Recognizing that its original approaches were not working, Germany decided to pursue a course that would make it more attractive economically. With proper follow-through, the nation can become one of the world's primary sources of direct investment and maintain its status as one of the world's preeminent exporters.

1"

Economic Realities

The German economy is the third largest in the world. Despite this strength, the nation faces a unique problem: how to bring its eastern area up to the western area's standards after forty-five years of Communist rule in the east. According to the *World Factbook*, western Germany accounts for 90% of overall German GDP and has three times the per capita income of eastern Germany (Central Intelligence Agency [CIA], 1996).

German citizens have a secure social safety net with substantial unemployment, health, and

---

Full title repeated on first page only.

Introduces topic and key question.

Short thesis, answers question.

Primary heading, centered, helps readers follow the argument.

Citation of source for all the information in this paragraph.

educational benefits. This safety net plus the
free market comprise what Germany calls a "social
market" economy (Eidson, 1992, p. 122). The west's
generous social welfare system was extended to
eastern Germany at reunification. Since 1990,
government transfers to eastern Germany have meant
ballooning public-sector deficits and borrowing.
To deal with these problems, the German government
decided to work on narrowing the federal budget
deficit for 1997. These efforts included cutting
back parts of the state's role in the economy
through privatization of formerly government-run
enterprises.

Currency Issues

The deutschemark (DM) is Germany's exchange
currency until January 2002, when the euro will
be introduced. According to the U.S. State
Department's country report (1997), Germany
participates in the exchange rate mechanism of
the European Monetary System (EMS). Against
non-EMS currencies, the value of its freely
convertible currency floats and has done so for
the past ten years. How the euro will affect
exchange rates remains to be seen. However,
exchange rate movements over a five-year period
indicate that the DM is strengthening against the
dollar (CIA, 1996). As shown in Figure 1, the
DM strengthened from about DM1.66/$ in 1991 to
DM1.53/$ in 1995.

APA in-text citation: author, date, and, for specific information, page number.

Point of figure is stated before figure is presented; figure is placed close to where it is discussed in the text.

Germany's Path 5

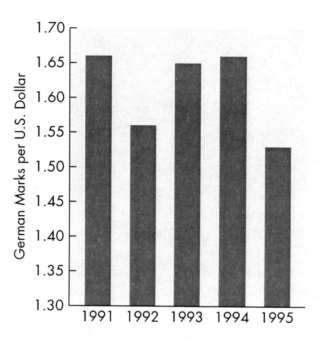

Figure 1 Direct exchange rate, 1991–1995: German marks per U.S. dollar. *Note*. The data are from *The World Factbook*, by the Central Intelligence Agency, 1996, retrieved November 1, 1997, from http://www.odci.gov/cia/publications/factbook/gm.htm

Foreign Direct Investment and International Trade

　　German foreign direct investment (FDI), as represented by the purchase of real business capital in other countries, has been primarily influenced by German integration into the European Union (EU). Also, trade between Germany and Central Europe has increased, partly because transaction costs are significantly lower for countries that are geographically close as well as for those within the EU.

But even though Germany's industrial/technical focus attracts foreign firms, FDI inflows have been lower than expected overall. As Agarwal (1997) points out, some factors that account for the low inflows include Germany's stringent environmental regulations, high corporate income taxes as well as wage costs, and rigid labor laws regulating hiring and firing. Germany's outflow, on the other hand, is quite high. Germany is the fourth most important global investor and is by far the biggest investor in such Central European countries as Hungary, the Czech Republic, and Slovenia (Agarwal, 1997).

Given its $1.9 trillion economy, the largest in Europe, Germany has an important role to play in trade relations with other countries, industrialized and developing (Fisher, 1995). Figures 2 and 3 show that Germany imports goods from its primary export recipients and that the countries of the EU are Germany's primary trading partners.

Germany's trade balance (surplus of merchandise exports over imports) has been somewhat more predictable than the economy as a whole. Trade balances have consistently increased over the years and reflect Germany's export-oriented economy. The increase was more dramatic in some years than in others, as data tabulated by Redman (1996) indicate. Between 1992 and 1993, for example, the trade balance increased by almost

---

Support by key facts (*see p. 32*).

Figures introduced and commented on.

Germany's Path   7

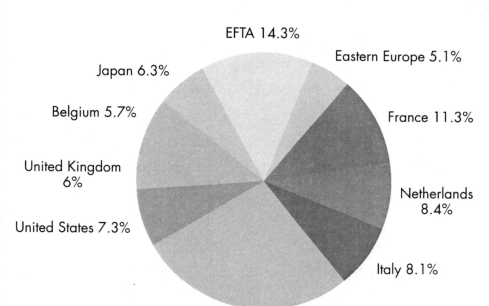

EFTA 14.3%

Eastern Europe 5.1%

Japan 6.3%

France 11.3%

Belgium 5.7%

United Kingdom
6%

Netherlands
8.4%

United States 7.3%

Italy 8.1%

Others 27.5%

Imports and Exports

Figure 2 Germany: Percentages of total imports from European countries, the United States, Japan, and other countries (1993). *Note.* From *The World Factbook,* by the Central Intelligence Agency, 1996, retrieved November 1, 1997, from http://www.odci. gov/cia/publications/factbook/gm.htm

DM30 billion. Between 1993 and 1994, it increased by only DM10 billion.

Economic Prospects

Many factors make Germany attractive both as a market for other nations and as a location for production. As the former east German citizens' standard of living increases due to reunification, their purchasing power and productivity increase. Intellectual property is well protected, and

Development by reasoning (*see pp. 25–26*).

Germany's Path   8

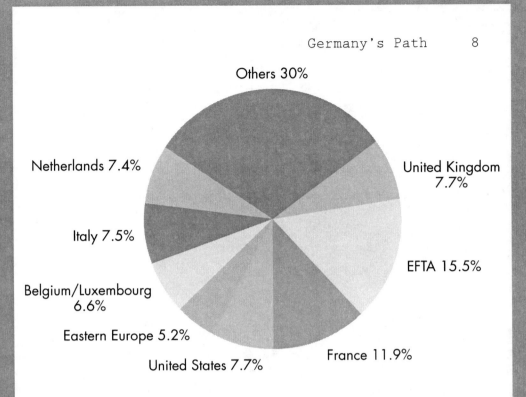

Exports

Figure 3 Germany: Percentages of total exports to European countries, the United States, Japan, and other countries (1993). EFTA stands for European Free Trade Association. *Note.* From *The World Factbook,* by the Central Intelligence Agency, 1996, retrieved November 1, 1997, from http://www.odci. gov/cia/publications/factbook/gm.htm

Germany is involved in most global treaties that protect business interests. Germany's highly skilled workforce is another plus for potential ventures and production plans. Generally, private enterprise, government, banks, and unions cooperate, making the country more amenable to negotiations for business entry or joint ventures.

Germany's Path   9

Germany also has an excellent physical location that makes it an "important crossroads for traffic between the North Sea, the Baltic, and the Mediterranean" ("Germany," 1996, p. 185). Equally important, a comprehensive and efficient transportation system allows businesses operating plants in Germany to transport their goods and services easily to other parts of the country and the world.

However, for the next few years, FDI will probably remain low because of high labor costs, high taxation, and government regulation. Recent government efforts to lower the tax burden on companies and consumers will help, as will the privatization of many publicly owned industries. According to Agarwal (1997), "privatisation related FDI often leads to reinvestments, and improves the climate for more FDI, reassuring investors about the continuation of liberal policies in the future."

During this period of restructuring, the DM might decline in value as foreign investors wait for change. But as Bindenagel (1997) points out, devaluation of the DM compared with the dollar and most other currencies should lead to a boost in exports and to accelerated economic growth:

> [E]xport growth will be an even stronger
> engine for growth in the next two years than
> expected, while growth in domestic demand

Quotation of more than 40 words indented 5 spaces.

remains moderate. Export orders remained
strong throughout December 1996, the trade
weighted DM dropped 3.9 percent . . . from the
middle of last year to February of this year,
and the prospects for growth in Germany's main
trading partners remain optimistic. (para. 16)
Continued export strength combined with the
eventual increase in inflows will result in
stronger economies in both east and west Germany
(Fisher, 1995).

Conclusion

All in all, Germany is experiencing a great
deal of change. In fact, it is remarkable that
just eight years after the fall of the Berlin
Wall, the German economy is working so well. If
the government efforts continue, the economy will
strengthen over the next decade, and Germany will
reinforce its position in the global economy. High
unemployment, high wages, high taxes, and the high
cost of doing business, especially in the east,
will continue to challenge economists and
government planners. Germany's path to continuing
prosperity depends on a national will to encourage
foreign investment. Economic advancement will not
occur without obstacles, but given Germany's
position at the crossroads of Europe, we can have
confidence in the nation's economic progress.

Germany's Path   11

References

Agarwal, J. P. (1997, April). European integration
and German FDI: Implications for domestic
investment and central European economies.
National Institute Economic Review. No. 160.
Retrieved November 1, 1997, from InfoTrac
(General BusinessFile ASAP) database.

Bindenagel, J. D. (1997). *Germany—Economic trends.*
U.S. Department of Commerce, International
Trade Administration. Retrieved November 5,
1997, from DIALOG database. (IT Market
IMI970409)

Central Intelligence Agency. (1996). Germany. In
The world factbook. Retrieved November 1,
1997, from http://www.odci.gov/cia/
publications/factbook/gm.htm

Eidson, J. R. (1992). Germans. In *Encyclopedia of
world cultures* (Vol. 4, pp. 121–124). Boston:
G. K. Hall.

Fisher, B. (1995). *U.S. global trade outlook:
Germany* (Office of European Union and Regional
Affairs Report). Retrieved November 7, 1997,
from http://tradeport.org/ts/ntdb/usgto/
selcoun.html

Germany. (1995). In S. P. Parker (Ed.), *World
geographical encyclopedia* (Vol. 4, pp.
180-187). New York: McGraw-Hill.

New page,
heading
centered.

Entries in
alphabetical
order and
double-spaced.

Hanging
indent, 5
spaces
or ½".

Germany's Path   12

Redman. (1996). *Germany—Balance of payment
    statistics.* U.S. Department of Commerce,
    International Trade Administration. Retrieved
    November 5, 1997, from DIALOG database. (IT
    Market IM960611.008)

U.S. Department of State. (1997). *Germany: Economic
    policy and trade practices, 1996.* Retrieved
    November 7, 1997, from http://tradeport.org/
    ts/countries/germany.html

Building Teams and Work Groups

Learning Points

How do I:

- Form a team and help it progress through developmental stages?
- Form or join a high-performance work team?
- Ensure that all members of a team contribute equally?
- Handle differences in values and work styles in a team setting?
- Allocate team roles and responsibilities?
- Motivate a team to achieve its objectives?

Jeremy was perplexed. He had been looking forward to the first team project in his new job. He had heard how much his new employer valued teamwork. At his previous job, he hadn't encountered teams. He had done virtually all his work on his own, as an individual contributor. This job was going to be different.

At the outset of the project, the group was given a series of projects on which to work. Over the course of the quarter, the group was supposed to evolve into what the team leader called a high-performance work team. But now, at the project's midpoint, Jeremy felt his group was anything but high-performance. Things had started out great. Right away, Jeremy hit it off with his fellow teammates. While the team was diverse in terms of gender, ethnicity, and function, most members had similar interests and got along well with each other. They had even gotten together socially a couple of times during the quarter. At the beginning, the group was very task oriented. They seemed to communicate well and were able to clarify their objective, determine their topic and research priorities, allocate roles and responsibilities, and set up a planning schedule working backwards from their project due date at the end of the quarter.

After a few initial organizing meetings, the group members were left to work on their own. That's where the problems started occurring. In preparation for an interim project due date, Jeremy and his team had planned a team meeting the day before to combine everyone's work and produce the deliverable that the team leader expected the next day. To his chagrin, Jeremy discovered that only he and one other team member were ready. The others had procrastinated and thought they could "wing it." He was contemplating pulling an all-nighter to make up the others' work. "This project is going nowhere," he thought. "Why didn't I just do everything on my own? I could have done better working on my own. This team stuff isn't all it's cracked up to be."

1. What is the situation Jeremy faces? What are the core issues here?

2. How did this situation develop? What could have been done to achieve a different outcome?

3. How would you feel if you were Jeremy? Has a similar situation happened to you?

4. What would you do if you were Jeremy?

5. What should Jeremy do?

"We are a pack animal. From earliest times we have used the strength of the group to overcome the weakness of the individual. And that applies as much to business as to sport."[1]

Tracey Edwards
(Skippered the First Women's
Crew to Circumnavigate
the Globe)

From the popular NBC reality show *The Apprentice* to most of the *Fortune* 500 and many high-tech start-up firms to competitive sports, teams are an everyday occurrence in our personal and work lives. As the nature of work progresses from individually based work to group settings, understanding teams and how to work in team settings and in work groups has become a crucial interpersonal skill. Not everyone is convinced that teams are more effective than individuals working on their own. But the reality is that many organizations are attempting to set up a team-based structure when tackling particular issues or processes, and the ability to work as a team is one of the most commonly required skills in the work environment.[2]

This chapter covers the basics of teamwork. We define teams and detail their importance in business today. We discuss strategies for forming teams and tips for making teams effective and successful. We also include several exercises at the end of the chapter for you to further enhance your team skills, and list resources available for further exploration.

What Is Teamwork?

A team is a formal work group consisting of people who work together to achieve a common group goal.[3] The word *team* is not synonymous with *group*. A **group** is a collection of people who work together but aren't necessarily working collectively toward the same goal. A **team** is composed of three or more interdependent individuals who are consciously working together to achieve a common objective, such as product development, service delivery, or process improvement. A group becomes a team when members demonstrate a commitment to each other and to the end goal toward which they are working. In a team, there is a higher degree of cohesiveness and accomplishment than in a group.[4]

From earliest times, human beings have used teams or groups to overcome the limitations of individuals. Collections of nomads in search of food and land, kingdoms composed of villagers and their leaders, native settlements, wagon trains and pioneers, the crews of ships—all were formed with the idea that more could be accomplished together than by an individual.[5] Even Adam and Eve decided to band together, as do the quasi-"alliances" on the CBS television show *Survivor*. Aside from gains in sheer horsepower, as in the case of a ship's crew, teams exist because few individuals possess all the knowledge, skills, and abilities needed to accomplish all tasks. Simply put, two heads are often better than one.

Within many professional sports teams, we can find shining examples of teamwork. Michael Jordan, one of the world's greatest basketball players and author of the book, *I Can't Accept Not Trying,* writes, "One thing I believe to the fullest is that if you think and achieve as a team, the individual accolades will take care of themselves. Talent wins games, but teamwork and intelligence win championships." He says he never forgot that he was only one-fifth of the effort at any time.[6] Staying with sports for a moment, consider the differences between a gymnastics team and a football team. In gymnastics, the members of a team may work together, but the ultimate achievement of a team is based on the collective efforts of the individual gymnasts. A winning team has the highest combined score. In football, a great quarterback is nothing without a great wide receiver, tight end, or offensive line that can keep him or her from getting sacked. The football team wins when all members work interdependently toward the same goal—passing and rushing their way toward touchdowns.

Returning to the workplace, it is estimated that between 70 and 82 percent of U.S. companies use the team concept, making teamwork skills one of the most commonly required skills in the work environment.[7] Many businesses are adopting a collaborative management approach that encourages sharing ideas and strategies throughout the organization. This collaboration provides many benefits to the organization as well as to the individuals who make up the teams.[8]

Why Teams?

Teaming is more than a phase or a buzzword. If it didn't work, organizations would abandon this strategy for getting work done. There is much evidence that teams can be effective, especially when tasks are complex and task interdependence is high. It is not always appropriate, of course, for work to be done in teams. But when a team structure is employed, and those teams work effectively, many benefits accrue to the organization and to the team members themselves.

Benefits of Teams

- Increased creativity, problem solving, and innovation.
- Higher-quality decisions.
- Improved processes.
- Global competitiveness.
- Increased quality.
- Improved communication.
- Reduced turnover and absenteeism and increased employee morale.

■ *Increased creativity, problem solving, and innovation:* Bringing together a group of individuals who possess a wealth of ideas, perspectives, knowledge, and skills can result in a synergy through which new ideas can be entertained. We each have a unique set of skills. Working with others allows us to combine our skills and talents to create new approaches to solving problems.[9] An example is a team of marketers where each person applies his or her strengths to the issue at hand. One person who is very creative can lead the process of coming up with ideas; another who is detail-oriented can do the initial research; a third person who is skilled in graphic applications can put together a great sales presentation.

■ *Higher-quality decisions:* Teamwork enhances the quality of the outcomes. Teamwork involves the collective effort of a group of people who represent diverse backgrounds and experiences. As more ideas are produced and alternatives are considered, the team gets closer to optimal decisions—decisions that are stronger because they have been made with various perspectives and interests in mind.

■ *Improved processes:* Teamwork results in a systematic approach to problem solving. Because of the necessary coordination between and transfer of learning among team members, teamwork results in organized approaches to the situation at hand. For example, a team is more likely than an individual to set up project checkpoints and planning systems to enable all team members to contribute to the project as it unfolds. Teamwork also permits distribution of workloads for faster and more efficient handling of large tasks or problems.[10] When members representing different organizations work together to improve a process that cuts across multiple organizational functions, more glitches and interdependencies will be uncovered and addressed than would be by individuals working independently.

■ *Global competitiveness:* Teamwork enables companies to compete globally. Firms in the United States are relying increasingly on diverse teams to compete in the global economy.[11] Diverse teams have skill sets and perspectives that are superior to what a single individual can bring to the table. For example, when Clairol marketed its popular Mist Stick in parts of Germany, it flopped. Had the Clairol marketing team included someone of German origin, they could have informed the group that *mist* was a slang word for "manure." As we continue developing and marketing our products in a global marketplace, combining diverse perspectives is essential.

■ *Increased quality:* Studies show that those large, complex, global companies that have moved to teams show increases in productivity, employee ownership of and accountability for their work, timeliness, efficiency, and customer service.[12] This results in higher-quality standards than are possible when individuals or groups of individuals, who lack a common goal, are doing the work.

■ *Improved communication:* The use of teams in the workplace enhances employee communication. In a traditional, hierarchical organization, communication tends to flow primarily in one direction—downward. In a team-based organization, communication flows laterally, upward, downward, and even outside the organization's boundaries (e.g., customers and suppliers). Teamwork requires collective action that is grounded in words and actions. It's not sufficient for one person to determine how he or she wants to work. Each person must get others on board before proceeding. In effective teams, there is rich sharing of information and ideas that improves communication within the team and between the team and the organization.[13]

■ *Reduced turnover and absenteeism and increased employee morale:* Teamwork results in changes in employee behaviors and attitudes. Teamwork fosters a camaraderie that helps many employees to feel more a part of the organization than when working independently. They feel ownership of the problems on which they work, get immediate feedback from teammates, see the fruits of their labors, and feel they have an impact on their job and the organization. Compared with the alienation employees often experience in traditional firms, employees in team-based organizations are happier, more committed, and more loyal to their organization.

The chart below contains examples of the positive outcomes that resulted when organizations embraced and encouraged team-based work:

Examples of Successes by Self-managed Teams[14]

Organization	Reported Successes
Harley-Davidson	Returned to profitability in six years.
Hallmark	200 percent reduction in design time. Introducing 23,000 new card lines each year.
Liberty Mutual	50 percent reduction in contract process time. Saving of more than $50 million per year.
Johns Hopkins Hospital	Patient volume increased by 21 percent. Turnover reduced, absenteeism reduced by 20 percent.
Monsanto	Quality and productivity improved by 47 percent in 4 years.
Saab and Volvo	4 percent increase in production output. Inventory turnover increased from 9 to 21 times a year.

Potential Limitations of Teams

While this chapter focuses primarily on the effectiveness of teams and work groups and how-tos for being a productive team member, there are some concerns about teams and their ability to make the most effective decisions. Some of these concerns are expressed briefly below.

Limitations of Teams

■ **Groupthink. Groupthink**[15]—or individuals agreeing reluctantly with a group's decision—is a potential problem for teams. Groupthink can happen when a decision is made in a hurry, when one or a few members are extremely dominant in a group setting, or when one or more members present believe they haven't had a chance to air their concerns before an action is taken.

■ **Social loafing.** By definition a team is a collection of three or more people. Invariably, a team will be composed of members with different work ethics and work styles, and this can result in some individuals doing more work than others.

■ *Quality concerns.* Ironically, although there is much evidence that teams produce quality outcomes, the fact is that some individuals have the expert knowledge necessary to be able to make decisions independently without the benefit of a team.

■ *Timeliness.* Individuals can make decisions more quickly than teams, especially if gaining buy-in from others is not an essential component of the action under consideration.

■ *Diversity.* In general, diversity of background and thought process is a good way to ensure that multiple perspectives will be incorporated into a particular decision. Sometimes, especially when expedience is desired or when management has a clear preference for a particular course of action, a homogenous group can make decisions more quickly and easily than can a more diverse group.

Organizing work into teams is the wave of the future. In fact, many organizations now have "virtual teams," in which much or all of the work is done by group members who may be dispersed geographically and communicate with each other primarily via e-mail and the Internet. But like any new phenomenon, it is important to understand that teams have both upsides and downsides. Teams may not be optimal for every business situation. When you are placed in a team, be aware of the potential problems and develop strategies early on to overcome these challenges.

Types of Teams

In the same way sports teams differ in function, makeup, and ultimate goal or purpose, so do teams in the workplace. The more commonly used team types are described below.

Cross-functional Teams: These include members from various departments or business specialties such as marketing, information systems, communications, public relations, operations, human resources, accounting, finance, planning, research and development, and legal. Cross-functional teams are usually charged with developing new products or investigating and improving a companywide problem such as the need to increase speed and efficiency across departmental lines or the need to adopt a new companywide computer system. Cross-functional teams derive their strength from diversity. By including representatives from all or most of an organization's primary functional areas, the team can diagnose a problem from multiple perspectives simultaneously, ensuring that all relevant points of view are taken into account. This can speed up the problem-solving process and result in an outcome that the various departments affected by the change more readily accept.

Case in point: Prior to producing its LH line of cars, Chrysler followed what most would call a serial design process. Engineering would design a car and throw it over the wall to manufacturing. "We can't build this," manufacturing replied, and sent it back over the wall to engineering. This would continue for months or years until marketing was charged with marketing a car that no one wanted. From product inception to market, this process could take as long as six years or more. By that time, technologies were obsolete and other companies easily stole market share. Realizing this, Chrysler moved to a simultaneous, cross-functional team-based design process. Everyone who had a stake in or was affected by the design of a new product was on a team that hashed it out—together. This included people from marketing, sales, engineering, design, and many others. These meetings had conflict, but the conflict was actually helpful. Chrysler was able to reduce the cycle time from over six years to less than 18 months!

Another example of a cross-functional team is a top management team. In many large organizations, the CEO typically makes strategic decisions in collaboration with the leaders of the major functional areas. Even at this level in the organization, top management recognizes their individual strengths and weaknesses and the value that diverse perspectives can add when making key organizational decisions.

Self-managed Teams: These are "groups of employees who are responsible for a complete, self-contained package of responsibilities that relate either to a final product or an ongoing process."[16] Also known as self-directed, self-maintained, or self-regulating, self-managed teams are typically given a charge by senior management and then are given virtually complete discretion over how, when, and what to do to attain their objective. Self-managed teams are expected to coordinate their work without ongoing direction from a supervisor or manager. Self-managed teams set their own norms, make their own planning schedules, set up ways to keep relevant members and others informed of their progress, determine how the work is going to be accomplished, and are held accountable for their end product or "deliverable." Many of these teams are responsible for hiring, training, and firing team members. The flattening of organizational structures, resulting in less hierarchy and fewer managers, makes self-directed teams a popular concept in business today. Of course, it's not as if management flips a switch and a team becomes self-managing. It's a long process of team building and teamwork combined with sufficiently greater responsibility and accountability gained through the team's demonstrated capabilities and performance.

Task Force: This is an ad hoc, temporary project team assembled to develop a product, service, or system or to solve a specific problem or set of problems. Companies are always faced with the challenge of getting ongoing, day-to-day work done while utilizing available resources to work on various change processes or product innovations. For example, a technology company might designate a group to study the next wave in software development while others are maintaining and servicing existing software programs. Often task force members are individuals who have demonstrated interest or skill in the area being examined by the task force, so the members are enthusiastic about the project and its potential. The task force process is very common in business today. It is lower in cost than hiring an outside consultant or group of contract workers and allows for management to allocate resources at will to various projects as the needs of the company and the interests of its employees change.

Process Improvement Teams: These teams focus on specific methods, operations, or procedures and are assembled with the specific goal of enhancing the particular component being studied. Process improvement teams are typically composed of individuals with expertise and experience in the process being reviewed. They are assigned the tasks of eliminating redundant steps, looking for ways to reduce costs, identifying ways to improve quality, or finding means for providing quicker, better customer service.[17] Process improvement teams are often given training on problem-solving tools and techniques to help them map processes, identify root causes of problems, and prioritize potential solutions.

To analyze a system and make recommendations for changes, process improvement team members diagnose the current state of a process and chart how it occurs step by step. They review customer or internal data and collect data from other sources such as managers, competitors, and others as needed. They identify ways the process can be enhanced, make their recommendations, and sometimes assist the operating units involved in implementing the changes. Process improvement teams are usually temporary and disband once the process being studied has been changed to the satisfaction of management.

Team Developmental Stages

Groups typically pass through a series of stages as they grow and evolve into teams. Theorists postulate that a team goes in and out of at least five stages in its life cycle:[18] forming, storming, norming, performing, adjourning. This process is fluid—teams may revisit a stage, or skip one or more altogether. Each phase has distinguishing characteristics and presents particular challenges to team members and their managers.

Stage One—Forming

In this stage, a team is established to accomplish a particular task. Typically the group members will not know each other, and even if they do, there is a feeling of uncertainty and tentativeness because people haven't had a chance yet to get to know one another and set group objectives.[19] In the **forming** stage, members will engage in behaviors such as defining the initial assignment, discussing how to divvy up the necessary tasks, understanding the broad scope and objectives of the project, and learning about the resources (time, equipment, personnel) available to the team as it works to complete the project. In this stage, there is some testing by members of leadership roles, some discovery of personality similarities and differences, some initial disclosure, and usually relatively little progress on the task.

As a team member or team leader, your role in stage one is to encourage the group to establish its mission and purpose, set up a work schedule, get to know one another, and establish some initial norms for working together.

Stage Two—Storming

In this stage, a group experiences differences over factors such as direction, leadership, work style and approach, and perceptions about the expected quality and state of the end product or deliverable. As is true of any relationship, conflict is inevitable. Many couples feel bad when they experience their first fight, and teams are no exception. When the first conflict among group members emerges, some or all of the members begin to feel less enthusiastic about the group and might even doubt the group can come together and achieve its objective. There may be struggles over leadership ("my way is best"), power ("if you don't agree we'll leave you behind") and roles ("who appointed you chief?"). In the **storming** stage, feelings emerge such as resistance to the task or approach being taken by the group, resentment about differences in workload, anger about roles and responsibilities, and changes in attitude about the group or toward individual group members and concerns. Typically in the storming stage, the group is in conflict and chaos, as the group has not yet established ways to communicate about these differences. During this stage, few if any processes and procedures are in place, as the need for them wasn't anticipated due to the lack of prior conflict. All of this can result in arguing among members, emergence of subgroups, and disunity. If and when a group in which you are working enters this stage, what can you do?

In the storming stage, your role as a group member or leader is to refrain from taking sides. Encourage the group to develop communication channels. Help your group members focus on the task and not on personal differences. Promote an environment of open communication to ensure that the inevitable conflict is healthy and results in improved communication and commitment to the group's task. Remember that an appropriate level of tension motivates a team, but too much or too little can affect productivity.[20] If your group cannot resolve or work effectively with conflict, request the assistance of a trained process consultant or facilitator. A group that can't learn how to handle conflict may never achieve its deliverable.

Stage Three—Norming

In this stage, the group faces its issues, conflicts, and power and leadership struggles openly and directly. The members establish and adhere to patterns of acceptable behavior and learn to incorporate new methods and procedures into their working together. In the **norming** stage, members feel a new ability to express constructive criticism; they feel part of a working team and a sense of relief that everything will work out.[21] In this stage, members attempt to achieve harmony by avoiding unnecessary conflict, acting more

■ *Accountability:* High-performance team members understand for what (and to what degree) they and others are held accountable. The team receives the message from the organization that performance matters—that it makes a difference whether goals are achieved or not. Expectations are clarified, and members are held responsible as individuals as well as members of the team.[35]

■ *Reward structures:* High-performing teams are rewarded for team accomplishments in addition to individual recognition. Organizations that support the team concept organize their recruiting, training, development, sales, business development, strategic planning, compensation, performance appraisal, and promotion strategies to support and reward teamwork.[36] When these strategies don't match with or undermine team processes or philosophies, the organization sends a mixed message and members find ways to "game" the system—often at the expense of their team. If an individual team member who "saves the day" for the department is rewarded for individual behavior, it sends the message that collaboration is not as valued as individual contributions or heroics, even if management's rhetoric suggests teams are truly valued.

Tips for Effective Teams

As a member of a team, it is important to be self-directed and work for the betterment of your team. You and your team members will be working with minimal supervision, and it is everyone's responsibility to make the team work. As athletes have learned, if one team member doesn't come through, the quality and performance of the entire team is affected. Teamwork requires full dedication and participation by all members of the team.

The following tips can help make your next team experience more positive and successful.

■ *Be focused.* Cooperate with your team members in concentrating on the current issues they face. Cooperation builds trust and mutual respect. Be willing and dedicated to working toward the common purpose.

■ *Handle conflict directly* and be willing to compromise. Be willing to explore conflict in a constructive, win–win fashion. Stand up for things that are important to you, but don't insist on getting your way in every discussion. When working together, put personalities aside and confront issues that arise. Resolve conflicts and walk away from sessions with regard, respect, and esteem for yourself and your team members.[37]

■ *Focus on both process and content.* Pay attention to the *process* of becoming and working together as a team as well as the *result* or end goal expected from the team. Teamwork is more than producing a deliverable. It also entails the approach or process used when people are working together.[38] The ends don't necessarily justify the means if team members despise and lack respect for team members because of the way decisions and outcomes were rammed through when teams fail to use a consensus approach. At team meetings, review both the processes being used as well as the status of the project.

■ *Actively participate,* and encourage others to do the same. At the beginning of a project, talk about roles and responsibilities. Also talk frankly about team members' schedules and their availability to participate fully in the project. Set up checkpoints to ensure that all are contributing equally.

■ *Keep sensitive issues private.* At the beginning of a project, discuss the importance of confidentiality. All teams engage in discussions that could be hurtful if made public. Have a pact that private information and views shared will be just that—not relayed to others outside the group. "What's said in the room, stays in the room."

■ *Communicate openly and positively.* In order to have full team participation, and for the team to learn and develop, it is essential that team members do not embarrass, reject, mock, or punish someone for speaking up and sharing ideas and perceptions. Foster a climate of psychological safety in order to motivate members to participate, admit errors, and share ideas and beliefs openly and comfortably.[39]

■ *Take time to establish operating guidelines* and clarify expectations. Make sure everyone is present for initial discussions of roles, responsibilities, and operating guidelines. For these guidelines to work, it is best that everyone participate in establishing and agreeing to uphold them. Put them in writing and have everyone sign them.

■ *Monitor what's going on with the team.* Watch for reactions, nonverbal cues, level of participation (or lack thereof), and general changes in the group's dynamics. Develop observational skills to help the team reach its full potential. A side benefit of doing this is that you increase your own interpersonal skills as you try to set a tone that is conducive to all members enjoying and participating in the team experience.[40]

■ *Practice giving (and receiving) effective feedback.* Express support and acceptance by praising and seeking other members' ideas and conclusions. If you disagree with others' viewpoints, criticize ideas but not the people. Be specific about the ideas that concern you and accept others' concerns about your ideas.

■ *Work with underperformers* to keep them in the flow of the project and prevent them from becoming excluded from the group.[41] If slackers are an issue in your team, talk with them immediately, preferably one on one. Find out if there is a personal problem preventing the member from being more engaged. Offer to be supportive but don't carry the workload. Give that team member specific, manageable tasks and hold him or her accountable. If the underperformance continues, talk with your manager or instructor. The person may need to be removed from the group or reassigned to a different team.

■ *Energize the team* when motivation is low by suggesting new ideas, through humor or use of enthusiasm. Encourage a time-out, if one is needed, or suggest a work or coffee break.

■ *Be reliable and conscientious.* Respect other members by honoring deadlines, commitments, and project milestones.[42] If you are having difficulty making a deadline, don't wait until the last minute—discuss the problem immediately with a team member or with the team. There might be a different way of approaching it. It's easier for a team to be flexible when there is adequate time to review the situation and come up with a different plan.

■ *When needed, give direction to the team's work* by stating and restating the purpose of assignments, setting or calling attention to time limits, and offering procedures on how to complete the assignment most effectively.

■ *Be supportive of your team members.* Always ask how you can help. It's a great way to remind everyone you're a team with collective objectives, not a group of individual contributors competing against each other.

Why Teams Fail

A note of caution: for teams and teamwork to succeed, there must be ample time in which to complete an assignment. Also needed are adequate resources to achieve the stated objectives and full management support of the team's effort. While the concept of teamwork is prevalent in both work and nonwork settings, not all situations warrant or are conducive to teams. Teams may be faced with tight deadlines; merging of processes and responsibilities; technological challenges; mismatched skills and abilities; unresolvable personality clashes, styles, and behaviors; limited work or teaming experience; or power struggles. In these situations, or in cases where there is no interdependence or need for collaboration, teamwork is going to be difficult if not impossible. These issues should be addressed early so that modifications can be made if necessary.

For example, if a team lacks the proper skill sets, additional members or training sessions can be added. If a power struggle is unfolding, a facilitator can be appointed. Inexperienced team members can be assigned informal mentors or coaches. Sometimes, if it's in the best interests of an organization, a team can be disbanded altogether. Perhaps the mission wasn't clearly defined at the outset of a project and the team members find they are unable to devote the time necessary to do the job. Or perhaps management requested individuals to work on a team project but made no allowances for mandatory day-to-day tasks. In situations such as these, it's appropriate for the team to be reconfigured (or disbanded) so that the original objective can be attained through either a different team or a different approach. Oftentimes, teams ignore early problems—perhaps believing such problems can be overcome—and become dysfunctional.[43] Intervening early, in a proactive way, can turn a team around or cause the organization to consider other, non-team-based approaches to solving a problem.

How can you deal with team members who aren't performing? Following are some tips.

Dealing with Problem Team Members

■ **Absentee member:** A member can become distracted by a work or personal problem that prevents him or her from following through on commitments made to the team. In this case, the best strategy is to be direct immediately. Discuss the situation with the team member in a way in which the person does not feel he or she is being put on the defensive. Explain the problem and find out the team member's perception of the situation. Ask specifically if the team member still has the time necessary for the team. If not, part ways if possible. If this is not possible, determine a way for the team member to make contributions outside of the normal meeting times and make the person accountable for a specific segment of the work that limits reliance on the team.

■ **Social loafer:** As mentioned earlier, it is not uncommon for one or more persons on a team to be able to "hide" the fact they're not contributing. This typically happens when the team members' work ethics differ and one or more team members "step up to the plate" and take on additional responsibility to ensure the work gets done, effectively covering for the less productive team members. Work standards will always vary from person to person. A strategy for dealing with this is to raise the issue at the onset of the project. Divide the responsibilities and set up checkpoints to ensure each member is contributing roughly equally. If a discrepancy appears, try to quantify it and re-allocate the workload so all members are contributing roughly equally.

■ **Procrastinator:** We're all human, and a seemingly human tendency is to "put off until tomorrow what we should be working on today." This is particularly problematic for work teams. Teams are composed of individuals with different work schedules and work styles. Some people thrive on the pressure of imminent deadlines while others find waiting until the last minute to be overly stressful. In this situation it is best to do two things: (a) set up interim checkpoints, or minideadlines, to ensure the work progresses at a reasonable pace, and (b) be realistic when work schedules are drawn up and deadlines determined. Prior to establishing deadlines, ask all team members to check personal and work calendars to catch any problems before they occur. At each meeting reclarify the commitments that might affect a person's inability to adhere to a deadline set earlier. And build in some slack: set the final deadline for a few days before the *actual* deadline—just in case!

Teams may not be a cure for all that ails an organization. But, teams can be very effective if the team structure makes sense and members practice the suggestions outlined in the chapter. Other steps team members and their managers can take to improve the likelihood of team success are summarized in the chart below:

Tips for Managing for Outstanding Results

■ Care about the people you work with—understand them, know what's important to them, and be able to motivate them.

■ Don't worry about who gets the credit—emphasize team effort and rewards; use the "whatever is best for the team" approach.

■ Respect individual differences—accept individuals and work to emphasize strengths and minimize weaknesses.

■ Subordinate yourself to a higher purpose—keep the common goal in the forefront.

■ Know yourself—be aware of your strengths and admit your weaknesses; surround yourself with people who can compensate for your weaknesses.

■ Don't be afraid to follow—some of the best teams are those where the leader doesn't call all the shots.

Source: Stephen Covey, "Team Up for a Superstar Office," *USA Weekend,* Sept. 4–6, 1998, p. 10.

Summary

Workplaces in the United States and abroad have embraced teaming. This is no accident. Organizations that implemented work teams as a way to improve products, services, and processes have witnessed tremendous measurable benefits. Some of these benefits accrue because of synergies—the notion that teams produce more and better solutions than individuals—gained from combining various skill sets, perspectives, abilities, and work styles on a single team. Not all teams produce phenomenal outcomes. By understanding the normal phases of group development and ways to gain and maintain group productivity and motivation, you can help your teams reach their full potential.

Key Terms and Concepts

Absentee member	Performing
Adjourning	Process improvement team
Cross-functional teams	Procrastinator
Forming	Self-managed team
Group	Social loafing/loafer
Groupthink	Storming
High-performance team	Task force
Norming	Team

Endnotes

1. Quote by Tracey Edwards in "Teaming with Talent," by Jim White, *Management Today,* Sept. 1999, p. 56.

2. Lillian Chaney and Julie Lyden, "Making U.S. Teams Work," *Supervision,* Jan. 2000, p. 6.

3. Karl L. Smart and Carol Barnum, "Communication in Cross-Functional Teams: An Introduction to This Special Issue," *Technical Communication,* Feb. 2000, p. 19.

4. Kevin McManus, "Do You Have Teams?" *IIE Solutions,* April 2000, p. 21.

5. Jim White, "Teaming with Talent," *Management Today,* Sept. 1999, p. 56.

6. Harvey Mackay, "Get on the Team and Be a Winner," *Providence Business News,* August 16, 1999, p. 38.

7. Chaney and Lyden, "Making U.S. Teams Work."

8. McManus, "Do You Have Teams?"

9. Ibid.

10. Smart and Barnum, "Communication in Cross-Functional Teams."

11. Chaney and Lyden, "Making U.S. Teams Work."

12. Mohsen Attaran and Tai T. Nguyen, "Succeeding with Self-managed Work Teams," *Industrial Management,* July–August 1999, p. 24.

13. Larry Cole and Michael Scott Cole, "Teamwork is Spelled Incorrectly: Teamwork = Communication," *Communication World,* April 2000, p. 56.

14. Attaran and Nguyen, "Succeeding with Self-managed Work Teams." Reprinted by permission of the Institute of Industrial Engineers, 25 Technology Park, Norcross, GA 30092, 770–449–0461. Copyright © 1999.

15. Irving I. Janis, *Groupthink,* 2nd ed. (Boston, MA: Houghton-Mifflin, 1982).

16. Attaran and Nguyen, "Succeeding with Self-managed Work Teams."

17. David Rohlander, "Building High-Performance Teams," *Credit Union Executive,* March 2000, p. 36.

18. Bruce W. Tuckman, "Developmental Sequences in Small Groups," *Psychological Bulletin* 63 (1965), pp. 384–99. The stage theory of team development was first identified by Tuckerman. Subsequent research has found the stages occur in a slightly different order. While the original model is reflected in this chapter, some researchers have found that teams more likely progress through conforming before entering the storming stage. See R. E. Quinn and K. S. Cameron, "Organizational Life Cycles and Shifting Criteria of Effectiveness," *Management Science* 29 (1983), pp. 37–61. Also see K. S. Cameron and D. A. Whetten, "Perceptions of Organizational Effectiveness in Organizational Life Cycles," *Administrative Science Quarterly* 27 (1981), pp. 525–44.

19. Peter R. Scholtes, *The Team Handbook* (Madison, WI: Joiner and Associates, 1988).

20. John R. Myers, "What It Takes to Make a Team," *Purchasing,* Sept. 2, 1999, p. 91.

21. Scholtes, *The Team Handbook.*

22. Daniel C. Feldman, "The Development and Enforcement of Group Norms," *Academy of Management Review* 9, no.1 (1984), pp. 47–53.

23. Scholtes, *The Team Handbook.*

24. Rona Leach, "Supervision: From Me to We," *Supervision,* Feb. 2000, p. 8.

25. Ruth Wageman, "Critical Success Factors for Creating Superb Self-Managing Teams," *Organizational Dynamics,* Summer 1997, p. 49.

26. Rohlander, "Building High-Performance Teams."

27. Barry Ekman and Emmanuela Ginngregorio, "Establishing Truly Peak Performance Teams—Beyond Metaphoric Challenges," *Human Resource Management International Digest,* 11, no. 3 (2003), p. 2.

28. American Management Association, "HR Update: Creating Real Teamwork at the Top," *HR Focus,* Jan. 2000, p. 2.

29. Smart and Barnum, "Communication in Cross-Functional Teams."

30. Paulo Vieira Cunha and Maria Joao Louro, "Building Teams That Learn," *The Academy of Management Executive,* Feb. 2000, p. 152.

31. Renee Evenson, "Team Effort: Beyond Employees to Team, beyond Manager to Coach," *Supervision,* Feb. 2000, p. 11.

32. Chaney and Lyden, "Making U.S. Teams Work."

33. Avan R. Jassawalla and Hemant C. Sashittal, "Building Collaborative Cross-Functional New Product Teams," *The Academy of Management Executive,* August 1999, p. 50.

34. Cole and Cole, "Teamwork Is Spelled Incorrectly."

35. Russ Forrester and Allan B. Drexler, "A Model for Team-Based Organizational Performance," *The Academy of Management Executive,* August 1999, p. 36.

36. Becky L. Nichol, "Top Ten Reasons Teams Become Dysfunctional," *National Public Accountant,* Feb. 2000, p. 12.

37. Jassawalla and Sashittal, "Building Collaborative Cross-Functional New Product Teams."

38. Cole and Cole, "Teamwork Is Spelled Incorrectly."

39. Cunha and Louro, "Building Teams."

40. Myers, "What It Takes to Make a Team."

41. Ted Gautschi, "Strengthen Your Team," *Design News,* Oct. 18, 1999, p. 158.

42. Myers, "What It Takes to Make a Team."

43. Smart and Barnum, "Communication in Cross-Functional Teams."

Exercise 10–A
Bridge Building

Groups of four to six are tasked with creating a bridge out of the materials provided. You have 30 minutes in which to complete this task. When the project is complete or time is called—whichever comes first—your instructor will roll a ball across your bridge to ensure it meets the project specifications. Following this activity, discuss these questions in your group.

Questions

1. How did your group decide how to build the bridge? Did it make a plan or did it just start building?
2. Did anyone play a leadership role in the task? Explain.
3. What made building the bridge as a group, rather than as an individual, more difficult?
4. In what ways did the group make the project easier? Explain.
5. Was your group a group or team? Explain.

Exercise 10–B
The Story: A Team
Exercise

Read the instructions and story below and answer the corresponding questions. Next, complete the same task in your assigned group.

What Does the Story Tell?

Instructions

Read the following story and take for granted that everything it says is true. Read carefully because, in spots, the story is deliberately vague. Don't try to memorize it since you can look back at it at any time.

Then read the numbered statements about the story and decide whether you consider each one true, false, or questionable. Circling the "T" means you feel sure the statement is definitely true. Circling the "F" means you feel sure the statement is definitely false. Circling the "?" means you cannot tell whether it is true or false. If you feel doubtful about any part of a statement, circle the question mark.

Take the statements in turn and do not go back later to change any of your answers. Do not reread any of the statements after you have answered them.

Story

The owner of the Adams Manufacturing Company entered the office of one of his foremen where he found three employees playing cards. One of them was Carl Young, brother-in-law of foreman Henry Dilson. Dilson, incidentally, often worked late. Company rules did not specifically forbid gambling on the premises, but the president had expressed himself forcibly on the subject.

Statements about the Story

1. In brief, the story is about a company owner who found three men playing cards.	T F ?
2. The president walked into the office of one of his foremen.	T F ?
3. Company rules forbade playing cards on the premises after hours.	T F ?
4. While the card playing took place in Henry Dilson's office, the story does not state whether Dilson was present.	T F ?
5. Dilson never worked late.	T F ?
6. Gambling on the premises of the Adams Manufacturing Company was not punished.	T F ?
7. Carl Young was not playing cards when the president walked in.	T F ?
8. Three employees were gambling in a foreman's office.	T F ?
9. While the card players were surprised when the owner walked in, it is not clear whether they will be punished.	T F ?
10. Henry Dilson is Carl Young's brother-in-law.	T F ?

11. The president is opposed to gambling on company premises.	T F ?	
12. Carl Young did not take part in the card game in Henry Dilson's office.	T F ?	

Questions

1. What process did you use to come up with the group answers?
2. Did anyone act as a leader or facilitator in the exercise? Explain.
3. In what ways was it difficult to achieve a group decision?
4. Which behaviors blocked the group's process? Which ones helped?
5. What are the advantages or disadvantages of working in a group compared to working as an individual?

**Exercise 10–C
Case Study on Gaining
Appropriate
Membership on Teams**

This is the team's third meeting. The team's task, deliverables, and membership have been dictated by a steering committee that oversees the division's teaming efforts. Members represent different areas and management levels within the division. A new team member who missed the first two meetings enters the room. Let's eavesdrop:

SCRIBE: "Okay. Here's our agenda. Does this sound ok to everyone?"

NEW TEAM MEMBER: "Well, not exactly. I have a question regarding the team's task. I know I missed the first two meetings, but I'm unclear about our purpose. I mean, without a well-understood purpose, are we ready to talk about membership? I'm not even sure if I should be here!"

SCRIBE: "Well, I suppose we can add "team purpose" to the agenda. How much time should we allot?"

TEAM LEADER: (Feeling strained by all the necessary structure.) "Could we hold off with the agenda for a few minutes . . . I know we need the agenda, but I think we should talk about purpose for a few minutes at least; then we can get back to the regular agenda. She (the new team member) brings up a good point."

Some discussion ensues. It becomes clear that the team's purpose *is* unclear. Other additional information is revealed, such as the fact that there had been three other team members who, shortly after being appointed by the steering committee, decided to excuse themselves from the team. Also, the team leader brought a new person in (call her Possible New Member), who is not really a full-fledged member until the steering committee approves it.

SCRIBE: "Back to the agenda. Were there any corrections to the minutes? (No response.) Okay, now for today's meeting roles . . . oh, our timekeeper isn't here today."

NEW TEAM MEMBER: (Looking at Possible New Member) "Would you like to keep time?"

TEAM LEADER: "Well, we're not sure if she is an official team member yet. Remember, the steering committee hasn't okayed her yet. Should she keep time if she's not?"

NEW TEAM MEMBER: "What's the difference? And why do we need the steering committee's blessing? Let's just do it."

TEAM LEADER: "Actually, there are some other names, in addition to Possible Team Member, that we've submitted to the steering committee. After all, we've lost three people since the team began."

NEW TEAM MEMBER: "Do we need additional people? Why? Again, doesn't it depend on what we're trying to accomplish?"

Questions

1. Why is it important to clarify a team's purpose? Once the task is given, why is clarification necessary?

2. What role does this purpose play in defining team membership? Why do you suppose others have "excused themselves" from the team?

3. How effective is the team leader? Explain.

4. Meeting management techniques—using agendas, having a scribe and timekeeper—are intended to make meetings more effective. In what ways could these techniques have the opposite effect?

5. If you were asked to participate in this meeting, what would you do to get the process back on track? Explain.

**Exercise 10–D
The Case of the Take-Charge Team Leader**

You are a member of a team that is meeting for the third time. Your goal is to reduce the number and dollar amount of workers' compensation claims. The team consists of members from safety, human resources, legal, and medical (e.g., staff nurses and doctors) departments. The team leader—a senior level manager—demonstrates a "take-charge" approach in that he or she believes he or she knows more about the task and assignment than anyone on the team. Early in the team's existence, the leader shared a project mile-stone chart that the team accepted. While the group has kept up with its assignments and is working rather effectively, the team leader seems impatient with the team's progress. In fact, the leader would like to exert greater control over the team's activities because he or she already has supporting data from outside groups and departments about the task and wants to complete the project in record time. However, you and other team members are concerned that (1) there may be other issues that have not yet surfaced, and (2) if his or her ideas are accepted, one of the team members may lose his or her position in the firm.

Questions

1. What issues are at play? How would you feel in this situation?

2. If the leader is so capable, why do you suppose management created a team to address this particular (and highly visible) problem?

3. At this point, what would you do and why?

4. If no changes were made, what do you think the final outcome would be?

**Exercise 10–E
Reflection/Action Plan**

This chapter focused on teams in the workplace—what they are, why they are important, and how to improve your skill in this area. Complete the worksheet below upon completing all the reading and experiential activities for this chapter.

1. The one or two areas in which I am most strong are:

2. The one or two areas in which I need more improvement are:

3. If I did only one thing to improve in this area, it would be to: